Hodder & Stoughton

A MEMBER OF THE HODDER HEADLINE GROUP

ACKNOWLEDGEMENTS

The publishers would like to thank the following contributors:

Jo Shackleton	-	Unit One, *Short Stories*
Karen Blake and Lynette Newman	-	Unit Two, *The Language Factory*
Bernadette Fitzgerald	-	Unit Three, *A Vein of Poetry*
David Watkinson and John Rowley	-	Unit Four, *Decisions, Decisions*
Jo Shackleton	-	Unit Five, *Ernie's Incredible Illucinations*
Jean Moore and John Catron	-	Unit Six, *Dear Diary*
Denise Savage	-	Unit Seven, *Teamwork*

Edited by Kevin Eames

Copyright Text:
p6, *A Pair of Silk Stockings* by Kate Chopin; p7, *The Bellows of Fire* from 'The Garden of the Villa Mollini © Rose Tremain, 1987, published by Sceptre; p8, Extract three – *Through the Tunnel* from 'The Habit of Loving' © 1954 Doris Lessing. Reprinted by kind permission of Jonathan Clowes Ltd., London, on behalf of Doris Lessing; p8, Extract four – *The Flowers of Algernon* © Daniel Keyes; pp10–15, 30–31, *A Message From The Pig-Man* © Curtis Brown on behalf of the Estate of John Wain; pp16–19, 21–25, 27 *The Withered Arm* © Thomas Hardy, Macmillan General Books; p34, Letter taken from *Put It Right* © Violet Brand, published by Egon Publishers; p41, *Speak to the Earth* © Vivienne Watteville, published by Genres 1996; p42, Majorca text taken from *Thomson Family Friendly Holidays*, May–Oct 2000; p43, Mallorca text taken from *Thomson A La Carte – Holidays of Distinction*, May–Oct 2000; p47, text at bottom – *Black Beauty* by Anna Sewell; p48, top left – *The Darkness Under the Stairs* by Lance Salway, from 'Ghost Stories' published by Longman 1990; p48, top right – *The Rose-Tree*, published in 'English Folktales' ed. Neil Phillip, Penguin 1992; p48, middle – *The Adventure of the Spreckled Band* by Sir Arthur Conan Doyle, published in 'New Windmill Book of 19th Century Short Stories' by Mike Hamlin, reprinted with permission of Heinemann Educational Publishers, a division of Reed Educational & Professional Publishing Ltd; p48, bottom – *George's Marvellous Medicine* by Roald Dahl, Penguin; p49, *Please Mrs Butler* © Allan Ahlberg, *Malcolm* © John Hegley, *Survivor* © Roger McGough; pp50-51, from *Dracula Eye-Witness Classics* © Dorling Kindersley, 1997; p52, 'Space Suits and Space Walks' from *Travelling Space* by Sue Becklake © Quarto Children's Books Ltd., 2000; p69, 'Haiku' by Eric Finney from *This Poem Doesn't Have To Rhyme*, Penguin; p69, 3 line Irish Haiku from *Cat Among the Pidgeons* by Kit Wright (Viking Kestrel, 1987) © Kit Wright, 1984, 1987; p70, *Wolf* from 'Midnight Forest' by Judith Nicholls, published by Faber & Faber Ltd.; p71, *White Water* from 'Quieter Than Snow' © Berlie Doherty, published by HarperCollins; p74, *Reflections* © John Mole 1987, in 'Meet and Write' by Sandy and Alan Brownjohn, Hodder Headline plc; p78, *Granny Granny Please Comb My Hair* © Grace Nichols; p79, *Swans* by Nicholas Tomkins, in 'What Rhymes With Secret' by Sandy Brownjohn, Hodder Headline plc; pp100–101, 'When A Mountain Blew Its Top' reproduced by kind permission of The Daily Mail; Unit Five, *Ernie's Incredible Illucinations* from 'Plays Two' © Alan Ayckbourn, published by Faber & Faber Ltd; p133 & 137–138, *Zlata's Diary: A Child's Life in Sarajevo* by Zlata Filipovi, translated by Christina Pribichevich-Zori (Viking 1994, first published in France as *Le Journal de Zlata* by Fixot et éditions Robert Laffont 1993) © Fixot et éditions Robert Laffont 1993; p134–135, *The Secret Diary of Adrian Mole* © Sue Townsend, Methuen Publishing; p139, *The Diary of Catherine Dunbar* in 'Diaries, Journals and Letters'; p141, *Star Trek* © N. Archer; p142, *Look Who's Walking* © Simon Brett, published by Victor Gollancz; p143, *Ig and Tig's Trip To Earth* by Keith Brumpton, first published in the UK by Orchard Books in 1991, a division of The Watts Publishing Group Limited, 96 Leonard Street, London, EC2A 4XD; p143, *Fluke* © 1977 James Herbert; p156, *Whose Life is it Anyway?* © Brian Clark, Heinemann Educational Publishers; p158, *Goal!* front cover 11/08/99, *Computer Act!ve* front cover 12–25/08/99, *Mizz* front cover 11–24/08/99, *Smash Hits* front cover 11/08/99.

Copyright Photographs:
p36 Golf course © Mike Hewitt/Action-Plus Photographic; p36 Garden centre © Barry Mayes/Life File; p42 Beach © Michael T. Sedam/Corbis; p42 Family © Photodisc; p43 Pool © Michelle Chaplow/Corbis; p43 Harbour © Michelle Chaplow/Corbis; p50 Vlad Dracula © AKG Photo; p50 Quiet village, Borgo Pass & Local people © Discover Transylvania, www.enzia.com; p51 Bran Castle © Peter Wilson/Corbis; p51 Graveyard © Todd Gipstein/Corbis; p52 Man in space suit © 1996 Corbis. Original image courtesy of NASA; p55 Robert Browning © Bridgeman Art Library; p61 Gustav Doré's *Rime of the Ancient Mariner* © Mary Evans Picture Library; p61 *La Belle Dame Sans Merci* by John Keats © Bridgeman Art Library; p66 William Blake's *The Tyger* © Bridgeman Art Library; p67 William Blake's *The Lamb* © Bridgeman Art Library; p85 Battery Unit © Jeremy A. Horner, Hutchison Library; p97 © The Red House; p100 Volcano erupting © Robert Francis, Robert Harding Picture Library; p101 Volcano © Sylvia Cordaiy Photo Library Ltd.; p137 Injured woman © Topham Picturepoint.

Orders: please contact Bookpoint Ltd, 130 Milton Park, Abingdon, Oxon OX14 4SB. Telephone: (44) 01235 827720, Fax: (44) 01235 400454. Lines are open from 9.00am - 6.00pm, Monday to Saturday, with a 24 hour message answering service. Email address: orders@bookpoint.co.uk

British Library Cataloguing in Publication Data
A catalogue record for this title is available from the British Library

ISBN 0 340 77537 8

First published 2001
Impression number 10 9 8 7 6 5 4 3 2 1
Year 2006 2005 2004 2003 2002 2001

Typeset and page design by Christopher Halls, Mind's Eye Design, Lewes, England.
Printed in Italy for Hodder & Stoughton Educational, a division of Hodder Headline Plc, 338 Euston Road, London NW1 3BH.

INTRODUCTION

Welcome to *New Hodder English*. This course book and its two companions represent a quality English curriculum for Key Stage 3 (S1-3). It addresses objectives in the National Strategy Framework for the Teaching of English at Key Stage 3 and promotes an interactive teaching approach essential to raising standards. It meets the demands of the revised National Curriculum Programme of Study (and Scottish 5-14 guidelines) without compromising on range, quality literature and a progressive ethos. Reading, writing and speaking and listening are integrated. Particular efforts have been made to provide accessible older literature, gripping non-fiction and opportunities to foreground speaking and listening.

STRUCTURE OF THE BOOK

The book is comprised of seven units, which are arranged to establish, revisit and consolidate key skills. Over the period of a year, all teaching points are revisited in new contexts. This course provides a full curriculum for those who wish to use it that way, but it is also a flexible resource. The units can be enhanced with texts and materials that schools have found successful, or organised around existing programmes of work.

LANGUAGE SKILLS

Language skills are developed in three ways. Firstly, each coursebook contains a unit devoted directly to language skills, and all the others take as their topic a linguistic or literary focus. Secondly, every opportunity is taken to teach language conventions at the time they are required in context. At these points, the conventions are taught directly and explicitly. Thirdly, it is assumed that teachers will continue to support pupils by giving them feedback on the detail of their writing, and specific support is provided in the Help Boxes.

STRUCTURE OF UNITS

Each unit is prefaced by a statement of aims, so that pupils have a sense of why they are undertaking the work. The activities in the unit are designed to introduce new skills and knowledge, consolidate the key points of learning and then to explore and develop these key points. Most activities can be undertaken individually or in groups. As much room as possible has been left for teachers to organise the activities in their own way. Each unit concludes with suggestions for further work to extend the more able.

PROGRESSION

The coursebook has been designed to interest and develop pupils of a wide range of ability, and most schools will find it suitable for mixed ability classes. The intention is to provide a motivating and accessible way into the full curriculum for all pupils, and to establish, consolidate and extend a handful of key learning points in each unit.

ASSESSMENT

Teachers should continue to use their usual patterns of assessment and recording, though the organisation of the course in units does lend itself to periodic review and a focus for assessment. Each unit contains focal writing assignments which will form one important strand of assessment. Importantly, teachers will be able to assess how far pupils have learnt new ideas and been able to use them in their own reading, writing and speaking. In the end, this is the only real test of effective teaching and learning.

CONTENTS

UNIT ONE

Short Stories

By looking at different short stories and discovering how they work, you will develop your skills as:

SPEAKERS AND LISTENERS

by discussing in groups your preferences and predictions in certain stories
by improvising conversations of characters in the short stories

READERS

by reading and interpreting short stories and extracts
by identifying clues in the text which help the reader to build up a detailed understanding in a short space of time

WRITERS

by writing your own versions of the endings of short stories
by writing a short story of your own

You know what 'short' means, but what is a 'story'? Discuss this with your group for a few minutes and then make a list of the things that all stories have in common. When you have done this, turn the page and consider the elements of a short story...

WHAT IS A SHORT STORY?

A short story usually takes no more than a few hours to read so the author has to pack a lot into a short space. So, the story:

- has to get going quickly, with an intriguing opening
- it has to keep the reader guessing, to give them the urge to carry on
- it can only afford to have a few characters – no more than 2 or 3
- it does not have lengthy developments of characters
- it has to suggest the setting in a few vivid and well-chosen words
- it needs intense, suggestive language because there is no time for lengthy descriptions and explanations
- it develops just one central incident or idea, and begins close to its climax
- it is powered along by a strong, assured narrator
- it has a punchy, satisfying and even unexpected ending

OPENINGS

Here are four openings to short stories. Each opening establishes a main character and his or her feelings about their present situation. It also gives an idea of what that character hopes for in the future.

Extract One

Little Mrs Sommers one day found herself the unexpected possessor of fifteen dollars. It seemed to her a very large amount of money, and the way in which it stuffed and bulged her worn old *porte-monnaie* gave her a feeling of importance such as she had not enjoyed for years.

The question of investment was one that occupied her greatly. For a day or two she walked about apparently in a dreamy state, but really absorbed in speculation and calculation. She did not wish to act hastily, to do anything she might afterward regret. But it was during the still hours of the night when she lay awake revolving plans in her mind that she seemed to see her way clearly toward a proper and judicious use of the money.

A dollar or two should be added to the price usually paid for Janie's shoes, which would insure their lasting an appreciable time longer than they usually did. She would also buy so and so many yards of percale for new shirt waists for the boys and Janie and Mag.

She had intended to make the old ones do by skilful patching. Mag should have another gown. She had seen some beautiful patterns, veritable bargains in the shop windows. And still there would be left enough for new stockings – two pairs apiece – and what darning that would save for a while! She would get caps for the boys and sailor-hats for the girls. The vision of her little brood looking fresh and dainty and new for once in their lives excited her and made her restless and wakeful with anticipation.

Extract Two

The two things I cared about most in the world until this morning were my dog, Whisper, and the bungalow under the viaduct.

Whisper is black and white with black blobs round her eyes and my aunt Nellie Miller says she reminds her of a panda.

Whisper is a one-person panda. The one person she loves is me. She waits for me to get home from school with her nose in the letter-box flap.

The viaduct is about a mile from our house. In winter, I can't get to it before dark, but in summer I take Whisper there every day. Trains used to go over it, but the railway line was torn up before I was born, so I've always known it like it is now, which is like a roof garden of weeds.

On rainy days, I hardly stop on the viaduct to look at the bungalow, because down there in the mist and drizzle it looks a bit sorry for itself. But in the sunshine, you see that it isn't sorry for itself at all and that the people who live there give it so much love and attention, you can't imagine they've got time for normal life.

Despite what's happened and what may happen in the future, I still feel that if that bungalow was mine, I'd be one of the happiest people in Devon. The only thing I'd add to the garden would be a wall all round it to keep Whisper in, so that she couldn't roam off to the sea when I wasn't there and drown.

The sea's second on my list of places I like, except that the sea does something to me: it makes me long for things. I sit down on the beach and stare out at invisible France, and this feeling of longing makes me dreamy as a fish. One of the things I long for is for time to pass.

Extract Three

Going to the shore on the first morning of the holiday, the young English boy stopped at a turning of the path and looked down at a wild and rocky bay, and then over to the crowded beach he knew so well from other years. His mother walked on in front of him, carrying a bright-striped bag in one hand. Her other arm, swinging loose, was very white in the sun. The boy watched that white, naked arm, and turned his eyes, which had a frown behind them, towards the bay and back again to his mother. When she felt he was not with her, she swung round. 'Oh, there you are, Jerry!' she said. She looked impatient, then smiled. 'Why, darling, would you rather not come with me? Would you rather ...' She frowned, conscientiously worrying over what amusements he might secretly be longing for which she had been too busy or too careless to imagine. He was very familiar with that anxious, apologetic smile. Contrition sent him running after her. And yet, as he ran, he looked back over his shoulder at the wild bay; and all morning, as he played on the safe beach, he was thinking of it.

Extract Four

progis riport 1 – martch 5 1965

DR STRAUSS SAYS I SHUD RITE DOWN WHAT I THINK AND EVREY THING THAT happins to me from now on. I dont know why but he says its importint so they will see if they will use me. I hope they use me. Miss Kinnian says maybe they can make me smart. I want to be smart. My name is Charlie Gordon. I am 37 years old and 2 weeks ago was my birthday. I have nothing more to rite now so I will close for today.

progis riport 2–martch 6

I had a test today. I think I faled it, and I think that may be now they wont use me. What happind is a nice young man was in the room and he had some white cards with ink spilled all over them. He sed Charlie what do you see on this card. I was very skared even tho I had my rabits foot in my pockit because when I was a kid I always faled tests in school and I spilled ink to.

I told him I saw a inkblot. He said yes and it made me feel good. I thot that was all but when I got up to go he stopped me. He said now sit down Charlie we are not thru yet. Then I don't remember so good but he wantid me to say what was in the ink. I dint see nuthing in the ink but he said there was picturs there other pepul saw some picturs. I coudnt see any picturs. I reely tryed to see. I held the card close up and then far away. Then I said if I had my glases I coud see better I usally only ware my glases in the movies or TV but I said they are in the closit in the hall. I got them. Then I said let me see that card agen I bet Ill find it now.

I tryed hard but I still coudnt find the picturs I only saw the ink. I told him may be I need new glases. He rote somthing down on a paper and I got skared of faling the test. I told him it was a very nice inkblot with littel points all around the edges. He looked very sad so that wasnt it. I said please let me try agen. Ill get it in a few minits becaus Im not so fast somtimes. Im a slow reeder too in Miss Kinnians class for slow adults but Im trying very hard.

INTRIGUING OPENINGS

- Read each of the four openings.
- In each case, discuss how the writer makes you want to read on. Why does the writer start the story in this particular way?
- Try to predict what might happen in each of the stories, and pick out some sentences that make you think as you do.
- Discuss what you think makes a good opening and then make a list of these qualities.
- Which of these openings made you want to read on? Discuss with your group why you think this is.
- Write an opening of your own which will tempt readers of your own age. Write five or six sentences which have the qualities you want to find in a good opening. Exchange openings with other people and discuss how successful they are in arousing your interest. In the light of this discussion, revise your opening and write it up neatly for a wall display.

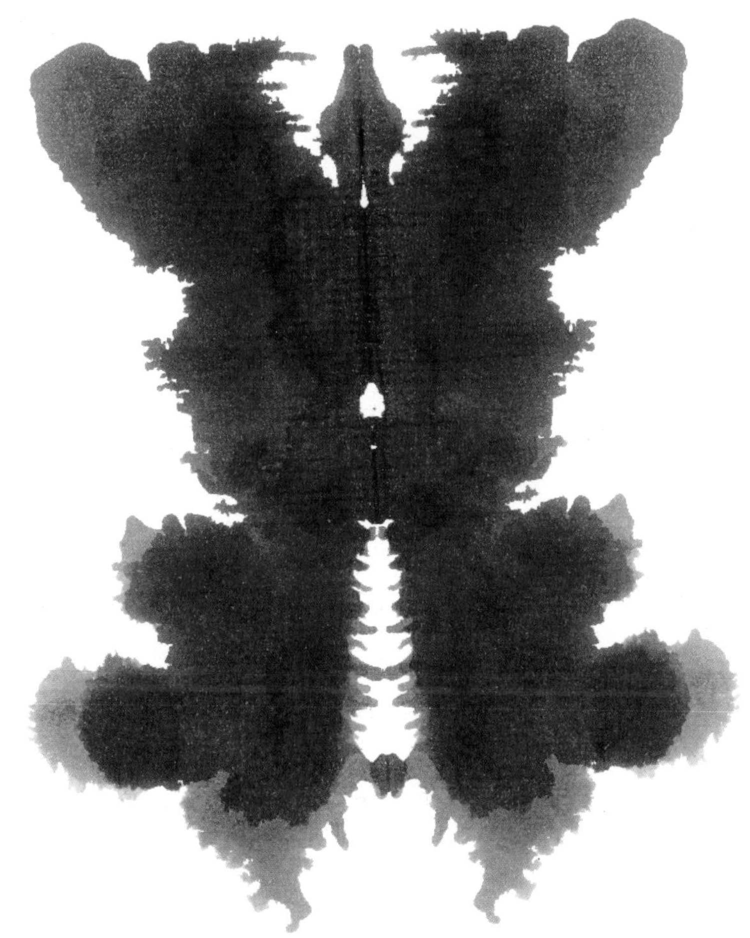

A MESSAGE FROM THE PIG-MAN *by John Wain*

He was never called Ekky now, because he was getting to be a real boy, nearly six, with grey flannel trousers that had a separate belt and weren't kept up by elastic, and his name was Eric. But this was just one of those changes brought about naturally, by time, not a disturbing alteration; he understood that. His mother hadn't meant that kind of change when she had promised, 'Nothing will be changed'. It was all going to go on as before, except that Dad wouldn't be there, and Donald would be there instead. He knew Donald, of course, and felt all right about his being in the house, though it seemed, when he lay in bed and thought about it, mad and pointless that Donald's coming should mean that Dad had to go. Why should it mean that? The house was quite big. He hadn't any brothers and sisters, and if he *had* had any he wouldn't have minded sharing his bedroom, even with a baby that wanted a lot of looking after, so long as it left the spare room free for Dad to sleep in. If he did that, they wouldn't have a spare room, it was true, but then, the spare room was nearly always empty; the last time anybody had used the spare room was *years* ago, when he had been much smaller – last winter, in fact. And, even then, the visitor, the lady with the funny teeth who laughed as she breathed in, instead of as she breathed out like everyone else, had only stayed two or three nights. *Why* did grown-ups do everything in such a mad, silly way? They often told him not to be silly, but they were silly themselves in a useless way, not laughing or singing or anything, just being silly and sad.

It was so hard to read the signs; that was another thing. When they did give you something to go on, it was impossible to know how to take it. Dad had bought him a train, just a few weeks ago, and taught him how to fit the lines together. That ought to have meant that he would stay; what sensible person would buy a train, and fit it all up ready to run, even as a present for another person – *and then leave?* Donald had been quite good about the train, Eric had to admit that; he had bought a bridge for it and a lot of rolling-stock. At first he had got the wrong kind of rolling-stock, with wheels too close together to fit on to the rails; but instead of playing the usual grown-up's trick of pulling a face and then not doing anything about it, he had gone back to the shop, straight away that same afternoon and got the right kind. Perhaps that meant *he* was going to leave. But that didn't seem likely. Not the way Mum held on to him all the time, even holding him round the middle as if he needed keeping in one piece.

All the same, he was not Ekky now, he was Eric, and he was sensible and grown-up. Probably it was his own fault that everything seemed strange. He was not living up to his grey flannel trousers – perhaps that was it; being afraid of too many things, not asking questions that would probably turn out to have quite simple answers.

ERIC'S STORY

- What have you discovered about Eric so far? First pick out all the factual information such as his age and name and make a list. Next pick out all the things you have worked out for yourself, even if they are not stated. For example, what has happened to his father? Make a note of phrases which give you clues about Eric and his feelings.
- The story is not told by Eric, but it does lead us to see events from his point of view. Go through the extract again and pick out some ways in which the writer has shown things from Eric's point of view.
- Try rewriting the opening few sentences to make the reader see events from the mother's point of view.
- Now read on:

The Pig-man, for instance. He had let the Pig-man worry him far too much. None of the grown-ups acted as if the Pig-man was anything to be afraid of. He probably just *looked* funny, that was all. If, instead of avoiding him so carefully, he went outside one evening and looked at him, took a good long, unafraid look, leaving the back door open behind him so that he could dart in to the safety and warmth of the house . . . no! It was better, after all, not to see the Pig-man; not till he was bigger, anyway; nearly six was quite big but it wasn't really *very* big . . .

And yet it was one of those puzzling things. No one ever told him to be careful not to let the Pig-man get hold of him, or warned him in any way; so the Pig-man *must* be harmless, because when it came to anything that *could* hurt you, like the traffic on the main road, people were always ramming it in to you that you must look both ways, and all that stuff. And yet when it came to the Pig-man, no one ever mentioned him; he seemed beneath the notice of grown-ups. His mother would say, now and then, 'Let me see, it's today the Pig-man comes, isn't it?' or, 'Oh dear, the Pig-man will be coming round soon, and I haven't put anything out.' If she talked like this, Eric's spine would tingle and go cold; he would keep very still and wait, because quite often her next words would be, 'Eric, just take these peelings', or whatever it was, 'out to the bucket, dear, will you?' The bucket was about fifty yards away from the back door; it was shared by the people in the two next-door houses. None of *them* was afraid of the Pig-man, either. What was their attitude, he wondered? Were they sorry for him, having to eat damp old stuff out of a bucket – tea-leaves and eggshells and that sort of thing? Perhaps he cooked it when he got home, and made it a bit nicer. Certainly, it didn't look too nice when you lifted the lid of the bucket and saw it all lying there. It sometimes smelt, too. Was the Pig-man very poor? Was he sorry for himself, or did he feel all right about being like that? *Like what?* What did the Pig-man look like? He would have little eyes, and a snout with a flat end; but would he have trotters, or hands and feet like a person's?

Lying on his back, Eric worked soberly at the problem. The Pig-man's bucket had a handle; so he must carry it in the ordinary way, in his hand – unless of course, he walked on all fours and carried it in his mouth. But that wasn't very likely, because if he walked on all fours, what difference would there be between him and an ordinary pig? To be called the Pig-man, rather than the Man-pig, surely implied that he was upright, and dressed. Could he talk? Probably, in a kind of grunting way, or else, how could he tell the people what kind of food he wanted them to put in his bucket? *Why hadn't he asked Dad about the Pig-man?* That had been his mistake; Dad would have told him exactly all about it. But he had gone. Eric fell asleep, and in his sleep he saw Dad and the Pig-man going in a train together; he called, but they did not hear and the train carried them away. 'Dad!' he shouted desperately after it. 'Don't bring the Pig-man when you come back! Don't bring the Pig-man!' Then his mother was in the room, kissing him and smelling nice; she felt soft, and the softness ducked him into sleep, this time without dreams; but the next day his questions returned.

IMAGINING THE PIG-MAN

- Try to draw a picture of the Pig-Man as Eric might imagine him.
- What do you make of Eric's disturbing dream? What does it reveal about his fears and hopes? Write a summary of your conclusions.
- Now read on:

Still, there was school in the morning, and going down to the swings in the afternoon, and altogether a lot of different things to crowd out the figure of the Pig-man and the questions connected with it. And he was never further from worrying about it all than that moment, a few evenings later, when it suddenly came to a crisis.

Eric had been allowed, 'just for once', to bring his train into the dining-room after tea, because there was a fire there that made it nicer than the room where he usually played. It was warm and bright, and the carpet in front of the fire-place was smooth and firm, exactly right for laying out the rails on. Donald had come home and was sitting – in Dad's chair, but never mind – reading the paper and smoking. Mum was in the kitchen, clattering gently about, and both doors were open so that she and Donald could call out remarks to each other. Only a passage lay between. It was just the part of the day Eric liked best, and bed-time was comfortably far off. He fitted the sections of rail together, glancing in anticipation at the engine as it stood proudly waiting to haul the carriages round and round, tremendously fast.

Then his mother called 'Eric! Do be a sweet, good boy, and take this stuff out for the Pig-man. My hands are covered with cake mixture. I'll let you scrape out the basin when you come in'.

For a moment he kept quite still, hoping he hadn't really heard her say it, that it was just a voice inside his head. But Donald looked over at him and said, 'Go along, old man. You don't mind, do you?'

Eric said, 'But tonight's when the Pig-man *comes*'.

Surely, *surely* they weren't asking him to go out, in the deep twilight, just at the time when there was the greatest danger of actually *meeting* the Pig-man?

'All the better,' said Donald, turning back to his paper.

Why was it better? Did they *want* him to meet the Pig-man?

Slowly, wondering why his feet and legs didn't refuse to move, Eric went through into the kitchen. 'There it is,' his mother said, pointing to a brown-paper carrier full of potato-peelings and scraps.

He took it up and opened the back door. If he was quick, and darted along to the bucket *at once*, he would be able to lift the lid, throw the stuff in quickly, and be back in the house in about the time it took to count ten.

One–two–three–four–five–six. He stopped. The bucket wasn't there.

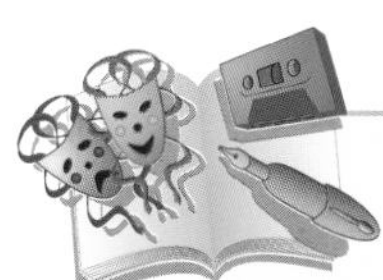

PREDICTING AN ENDING

- Discuss with your group what might happen next.
- Write your own ending of about one hundred words. Think carefully about how the characters have been portrayed. Try to write from Eric's point of view, as the author has done. Provide an unexpected but believable ending.
- Share your ideas with others in your class. Whose ending do you prefer and why? You can read the rest of the story at the end of this unit.

THE WITHERED ARM

The following short story was written by Thomas Hardy at the end of the 19th century. As it is a longer tale, parts of the story have been filled in for you.

A Lorn Milkmaid

It was an eighty-cow dairy, and the troop of milkers, regular and supernumerary, were all at work; for, though the time of year was as yet but early April, the feed lay entirely in water-meadows, and the cows were 'in full pail'. The hour was about six in the evening, and three-fourths of the large, red, rectangular animals having been finished off, there was opportunity for a little conversation.

'He do bring home his bride tomorrow, I hear. They've come as far as Anglebury today.'

The voice seemed to proceed from the belly of the cow called Cherry, but the speaker was a milking-woman, whose face was buried in the flank of that motionless beast.

'Hav' anybody seen her?' said another.

There was a negative response from the first. 'Though they say she's a rosy-cheeked, tisty-tosty little body enough,' she added; and as the milkmaid spoke she turned her face so that she could glance past her cow's tail to the other side of the barton, where a thin, fading woman of thirty milked somewhat apart from the rest.

'Years younger than he, they say,' continued the second, with also a glance of reflectiveness in the same direction.

'How old do you call him, then?'

'Thirty or so.'

'More like forty,' broke in an old milkman near, in a long white pinafore or 'wropper', and with the brim of his hat tied down, so that he looked like a woman. ''A was born before our Great Weir was builded, and I hadn't man's wages when I laved water there.'

The discussion waxed so warm that the purr of the milk-streams became jerky, till a voice from another cow's belly cried with authority, 'Now then, what the Turk do it matter to us about Farmer Lodge's age, or Farmer Lodge's new mis'ess? I shall have to pay him nine pound a year for the rent of every one of these milchers, whatever his age or hers. Get on with your work, or 'twill be dark afore we have done. The evening is pinking in a'ready.' This speaker was the dairyman himself, by whom the milkmaids and men were employed.

Nothing more was said publicly about Farmer Lodge's wedding, but the first woman murmured under her cow to her next neighbour, ''Tis hard for *she*,' signifying the thin worn milkmaid aforesaid.

'O no,' said the second. 'He ha'n't spoke to Rhoda Brook for years.'

When the milking was done they washed their pails and hung them on a many-forked stand made as usual of the peeled limb of an oak-tree, set upright in the earth, and resembling a colossal antlered horn. The majority then dispersed in various directions homeward. The thin woman who had not spoken was joined by a boy of twelve or thereabout, and the twain went away up the field also.

Their course lay apart from that of the others, to a lonely spot high above the water-meads, and not far from the border of Egdon Heath, whose dark countenance was visible in the distance as they drew nigh to their home.

'They've just been saying down in barton that your father brings his young wife home from Anglebury tomorrow,' the woman observed. 'I shall want to send you for a few things to market, and you'll be pretty sure to meet 'em.'

'Yes, Mother,' said the boy. 'Is Father married then?'

'Yes. . . . You can give her a look, and tell me what's she's like, if you do see her.'

'Yes, Mother.'

'If she's dark or fair, and if she's tall – as tall as I. And if she seems like a woman who has ever worked for a living, or one that has been always well off, and has never done anything, and shows marks of the lady on her, as I expect she do.'

'Yes.'

They crept up the hill in the twilight, and entered the cottage. It was built of mud-walls, the surface of which had been washed by many rains into channels and depressions that left none of the original flat face visible; while here and there in the thatch above a rafter showed like a bone protruding through the skin.

She was kneeling down in the chimney-corner, before two pieces of turf laid together with the heather inwards, blowing at the red-hot ashes with her breath till the turves flamed. The radiance lit her pale cheek, and made her dark eyes, that had once been handsome, seem handsome anew. 'Yes,' she resumed, 'see if she is dark or fair, and if you can, notice if her hands be white; if not, see if they look as though she had ever done housework, or are milker's hands like mine.'

The boy again promised, inattentively this time, his mother not observing that he was cutting a notch with his pocket-knife in the beech-backed chair.

GETTING INTO THE STORY

- Working in a group, go through the story slowly and write down what is happening in your own words.
- What impression do you have of the time and place in which the story is set? What details in the text give you this impression?
- What do you think might have happened in the past between Farmer Lodge and Rhoda Brook?
- Write a brief diary entry for a) Rhoda and b) her son for the day Farmer Lodge returns home with his young bride.
- Now carry on reading the story.

A Vision

One night, two or three weeks after the bridal return, when the boy was gone to bed, Rhoda sat a long time over the turf ashes that she had raked out in front of her to extinguish them. She contemplated so intently the new wife, as presented to her in her mind's eye over the embers, that she forgot the lapse of time. At last, wearied with her day's work, she too retired.

But the figure which had occupied her so much during this and the previous days was not to be banished at night. For the first time Gertrude Lodge visited the supplanted woman in her dreams. Rhoda Brook dreamed – since her assertion that she really saw, before falling asleep, was not to be believed – that the young wife, in the pale silk dress and white bonnet, but with features shockingly distorted, and wrinkled as by age, was sitting upon her chest as she lay. The pressure of Mrs Lodge's person grew heavier; the blue eyes peered cruelly into her face; and then the figure thrust forward its left hand mockingly, so as to make the wedding-ring it wore glitter in Rhoda's eyes. Maddened mentally, and nearly suffocated by pressure, the sleeper struggled; the incubus, still regarding her, withdrew to the foot of the bed, only, however, to come forward by degrees, resume her seat, and flash her left hand as before.

Gasping for breath, Rhoda, in a last desperate effort, swung out her right hand, seized the confronting spectre by its obtrusive left arm, and whirled it backward to the floor, starting up herself as she did so with a low cry.

'O, merciful heaven!' she cried, sitting on the edge of the bed in a cold sweat; 'that was not a dream – she was here!'

She could feel her antagonist's arm within her grasp even now – the very flesh and bone of it, as it seemed. She looked on the floor whither she had whirled the spectre, but there was nothing to be seen.

Rhoda Brook slept no more that night, and when she went milking at the next dawn they noticed how pale and haggard she looked. The milk that she drew quivered into the pail; her hand had not calmed even yet, and still retained the feel of the arm. She came home to breakfast as wearily as it if had been suppertime.

'What was that noise in your chimmer, Mother, last night?' said her son. 'You fell off the bed, surely?'

'Did you hear anything fall? At what time?'

'Just when the clock struck two.'

She could not explain, and when the meal was done went silently about her household work, the boy assisting her, for he hated going afield on the farms, and she indulged his reluctance. Between eleven and twelve the garden-gate clicked and she lifted her eyes to the window. At the bottom of the garden, within the gate, stood the woman of her vision. Rhoda seemed transfixed.

RHODA'S VISION

Discuss the following questions in your group.

- What do you make of Rhoda's disturbing dream? What does it suggest?
- How do you account for the boy waking up?
- Why do you think Gertrude Lodge has come to visit Rhoda?
- What sort of story are you now expecting this to be – a romance, a thriller, a comedy? Pick out some phrases or sentences that suggest your opinion is right.

In fact, Gertrude has come to offer new boots to replace the boy's worn out pair. She had met him the previous day, and felt sorry because he was so poor and bedraggled.

- Draw two outlines to represent Rhoda and Gertrude. Draw thought bubbles coming out of their heads of all the things they might be thinking and feeling at this moment. Remember that Gertrude is new to the neighbourhood and knows no-one.
- Now **improvise** the conversation which might take place between the two women.

HELP

Improvise – act out, without a set script or directions, using your imagination.

Mrs Lodge was by this time close to the door – not in her silk, as Rhoda had dreamt of in the bed-chamber, but in a morning hat, and gown of common light material, which became her better than silk. On her arm she carried a basket.

The impression remaining from the night's experience was still strong. Brook had almost expected to see the wrinkles, the scorn, and the cruelty on her visitor's face. She would have escaped an interview, had escape been possible. There was, however, no backdoor to the cottage, and in an instant the boy had lifted the latch to Mrs Lodge's gentle knock.

'I see I have come to the right house,' said she, glancing at the lad, and smiling. 'But I was not sure till you opened the door.'

The figure and action were those of the phantom; but her voice was so indescribably sweet, her glance so winning, her smile so tender, so unlike that of Rhoda's midnight visitant, that the latter could hardly believethe evidence of her senses. She was truly glad that she had not hidden away in sheer aversion, as she had been inclined to do. In her basket Mrs Lodge brought the pair of boots that she had promised to the boy, and other useful articles.

At these proofs of a kindly feeling toward her and hers Rhoda's heart reproached her bitterly. This innocent young thing should have her blessing and not her curse. When she left them a light seemed gone from the dwelling. Two days later she came again to know if the boots fitted; and less than a fortnight after that paid Rhoda another call. On this occasion the boy was absent.

'I walk a good deal,' said Mrs Lodge, 'and your house is the nearest outside our own parish. I hope you are well. You don't look quite well.'

Rhoda said she was well enough; and, indeed, though the paler of the two, there was more of the strength that endures in her well-defined features and large frame, than in the soft-cheeked young woman before her. The conversation became quite confidential as regarded their powers and weaknesses; and when Mrs Lodge was leaving, Rhoda said, 'I hope you will find this air agrees with you, ma'am, and not suffer from the damp of the water meads.'

The younger one replied that there was not much doubt of it, her general health being usually good. 'Though, now you remind me,' she added, 'I have one little ailment which puzzles me. It is nothing serious, but I cannot make it out.'

She uncovered her left hand and arm; and their outline confronted Rhoda's gaze as the exact original of the limb she had beheld and seized in her dream. Upon the pink round surface of the arm were faint marks of an unhealthy colour, as if produced by a rough grasp. Rhoda's eyes became riveted on the discolourations; she fancied that she discerned in them the shape of her own four fingers.

'How did it happen?' she said mechanically.

'I cannot tell,' replied Mrs Lodge, shaking her head. 'One night when I was sound asleep, dreaming I was away in some strange place, a pain suddenly shot into my arm there, and was so keen as to awaken me. I must have struck it in the daytime, I suppose, though I don't remember doing so.' She added, laughing, 'I tell my dear husband that it looks just as if he had flown into a rage and struck me there. O, I daresay it will soon disappear.'

'Ha, ha! Yes .... On what night did it come?'

Mrs Lodge considered, and said it would be a fortnight ago on the morrow. 'When I awoke I could not remember where I was,' she added, 'till the clock striking two reminded me.' She had named the night and the hour of Rhoda's spectral encounter, and Brook felt like a guilty thing. The artless disclosure startled her; she did not reason on the freaks of coincidence; and all the scenery of that ghastly night returned with double vividness to her mind.

'O, can it be,' she said to herself, when her visitor had departed, 'that I exercise a malignant power over people against my own will?' She knew that she had been slyly called a witch since her fall; but never having understood why that particular stigma had been attached to her, it had passed disregarded. Could this be the explanation, and had such things as this ever happened before?

THE EVIDENCE

- Do you believe that Rhoda could have caused the withered arm? What arguments can you see for believing it to be her fault? What arguments can you make in defence of Rhoda? Discuss your thoughts with a partner and then write a summary of your conclusions.
- How is the story going to develop from here, do you think? What kind of ending are you expecting? What helps us to sense the way a story is going to go?
- Now read on.

THE EVENTS THAT FOLLOW....

A Rencounter *(many years later)*

It was one o'clock on Saturday. Gertrude Lodge, having been admitted to the jail as above described, was sitting in a waiting-room within the second gate, which stood under a classic archway of ashlar, then comparatively modern, and bearing the inscription, 'COVNTY JAIL: 1793'. This had been the façade she saw from the heath the day before. Near at hand was a passage to the roof on which the gallows stood.

The town was thronged, and the market suspended; but Gertrude had seen scarcely a soul. Having kept her room till the hour of the appointment, she had proceeded to the spot by a way which avoided the open space below the cliff where the spectators had gathered; but she could, even now, hear the multitudinous babble of their voices, out of which rose at intervals the hoarse croak of a single voice uttering the words, 'Last dying speech and confession!' There had been no reprieve, and the execution was over; but the crowd still waited to see the body taken down.

Soon the persistent woman heard a trampling overhead, then a hand beckoned to her, and, following directions, she went out and crossed the inner paved court beyond the gatehouse, her knees trembling so that she could scarcely walk. One of her arms was out of its sleeve, and only covered by her shawl.

On the spot at which she had now arrived were two trestles, and before she could think of their purpose she heard heavy feet descending stairs somewhere at her back. Turn her head she would not, or could not, and, rigid in this position, she was conscious of a rough coffin passing her shoulder, borne by four men. It was open, and in it lay the body of a young man, wearing the smockfrock of a rustic, and fustian breeches. The corpse had been thrown into the coffin so hastily that the skirt of the smockfrock was hanging over. The burden was temporarily deposited on the trestles.

By this time the young woman's state was such that a grey mist seemed to float before her eyes, on account of which, and the veil she wore, she could scarcely discern anything: it was as though she had nearly died, but was held up by a sort of galvanism.

'Now!' said a voice close at hand, and she was just conscious that the word had been addressed to her.

PREDICTING THE ENDING

- Now predict the ending of the story. Find three clues in the story which support your idea, and discuss your conclusion with others in your group.
- Then read on.

By a last strenuous effort she advanced, at the same time hearing persons approaching behind her. She bared her poor curst arm; and Davies, uncovering the face of the corpse, took Gerturde's hand, and held it so that her arm lay across the dead man's neck, upon a line the colour of an unripe blackberry, which surrounded it.

Gertrude shrieked: 'the turn o' the blood,' predicted by the conjuror, had taken place. But at that moment a second shriek rent the air of the enclosure: it was not Gertrude's, and its effect upon her was to make her start round.

Immediately behind her stood Rhoda Brook, her face drawn, and her eyes red with weeping. Behind Rhoda stood Gertrude's own husband; his countenance lined, his eyes dim, but without a tear.

'D— you! what are you doing here?' he said hoarsely.

'Hussy – to come between us and our child now!' cried Rhoda. 'This is the meaning of what Satan showed me in the vision! You are like her at last!' And clutching the bare arm of the younger woman, she pulled her unresistingly back against the wall. Immediately Brook had loosened her hold the fragile young Gertrude slid down against the feet of her husband. When he lifted her up she was unconscious.

The mere sight of the twain had been enough to suggest to her that the dead young man was Rhoda's son. At that time the relatives of an executed convict had the privilege of claiming the body for burial, if they chose to do so; and it was for this purpose that Lodge was awaiting the inquest with Rhoda. He had been summoned by her as soon as the young man was taken in the crime, and at different times since; and he had attended in court during the trial. This was the 'holiday' he had been indulging in of late. The two wretched parents had wished to avoid exposure; and hence had come themselves for the body, a waggon and sheet for its conveyance and covering being in waiting outside.

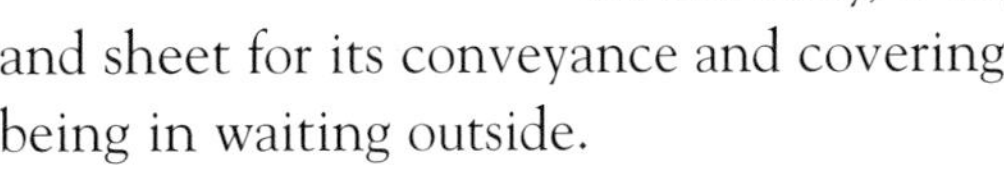

RETELLING *THE WITHERED ARM*

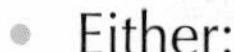

- Working in a group to represent each of the characters (Rhoda, her son, Lodge and Gertrude) take turns to retell the events in role from the point of view of each character. Stop after each telling to discuss who, if anyone, should carry the blame for all the sadness in the story.

- Which character do you most sympathise with and why?

- Either:

  Choose a scene in the story and rewrite it as a **first person narrative**, so that it is told by one of the characters, and expresses their thoughts and feelings about the events as they happen.

  Or: Write in story form about the events which you imagine took place before the opening of the story.

HELP

First person narrative – story told by one of the characters, using 'I'.

Or: Write about the events you imagine taking place after the close of the story, sketching out the life stories of those who survived.

You may then like to read the following epilogue that completes *The Withered Arm.*

AFTERWARDS

Some authors add a summary of what happened to the characters after the climax of the story. This is often needed to tie up loose ends and avoid leaving the reader bewildered as to what the outcome might have been.

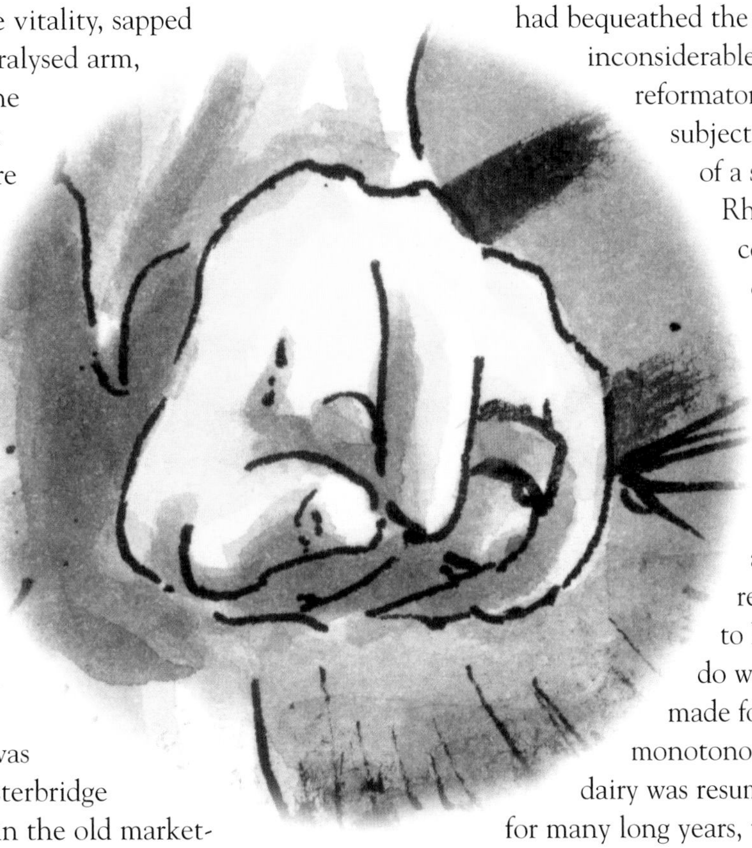

Gertrude's case was so serious that it was deemed advisable to call to her the surgeon who was at hand. She was taken out of the jail into the town; but she never reached home alive. Her delicate vitality, sapped perhaps by the paralysed arm, collapsed under the double shock that followed the severe strain, physical and mental, to which she had subjected herself during the previous twenty-four hours. Her blood had been 'turned' indeed – too far. Her death took place in the town three days after.

Her husband was never seen in Casterbridge again; once only in the old market-place at Anglebury, which he had so much frequented, and very seldom in public anywhere. Burdened at first with moodiness and remorse, he eventually changed for the better, and appeared as a chastened and thoughtful man. Soon after attending the funeral of his poor young wife he took steps towards giving up the farms in Holmstoke and the adjoining parish, and, having sold every head of his stock, he went away to Port-Bredy, at the other end of the county, living there in solitary lodgings till his death two years later of a painless decline. It was then found that he had bequeathed the whole of his not inconsiderable property to a reformatory for boys, subject to the payment of a small annuity to Rhoda Brook, if she could be found to claim it.

For some time she could not be found; but eventually she reappeared in her old parish – absolutely refusing, however, to have anything to do with the provision made for her. Her monotonous milking at the dairy was resumed, and followed for many long years, till her form became bent, and her once abundant dark hair white and worn away at the forehead – perhaps by long pressure against the cows. Here, sometimes, those who knew her experiences would stand and observe her, and wonder what sombre thoughts were beating inside that impassive, wrinkled brow, to the rhythm of the alternating milk-streams.

THE DRAFTING ROUTE

When you have made notes on the subject and style of your project, and when you have made a list of useful words or phrases to help you write it, you can begin drafting:

PLAN

Make a rough plan of your piece of writing, including ideas about how you will begin, what will be your theme and how you will end the piece.

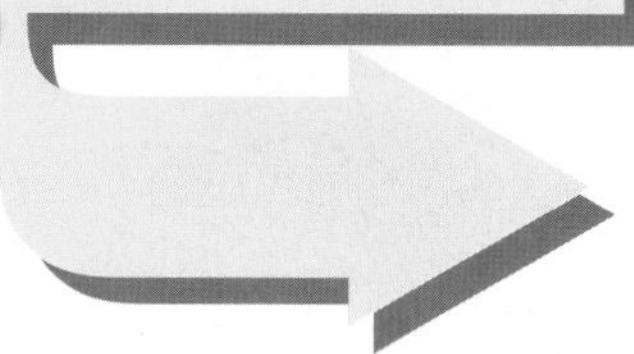

FIRST DRAFT

Write your first draft. Try to include all of the details you planned, keeping to the style in which you have chosen to write. Be careful with spelling and punctuation.

CHECK IT

Is it 'colourful' in description and does it contain enough details? How do you think it could be improved?

HAVE IT REVIEWED

Ask another member of your group to read your work and make constructive criticisms (review it), to help you see where you might improve it for your reader. Make sure you have a note of the points your friend makes.

FINAL DRAFT

Before you write your final draft, check any spellings you are unsure about in a dictionary, make sure that your punctuation is correct and gives the effects you want. Make any changes you need to, based on your reviewer's comments.

Write your final draft, making sure that your writing is clear. Your final draft may be illustrated and/or word processed. (Check that you have put your name on your piece of work.)

WRITING YOUR OWN SHORT STORY

Having looked at extracts from several short stories, you are now ready to write your own.

- Working with a partner, plan your ideas first like this:

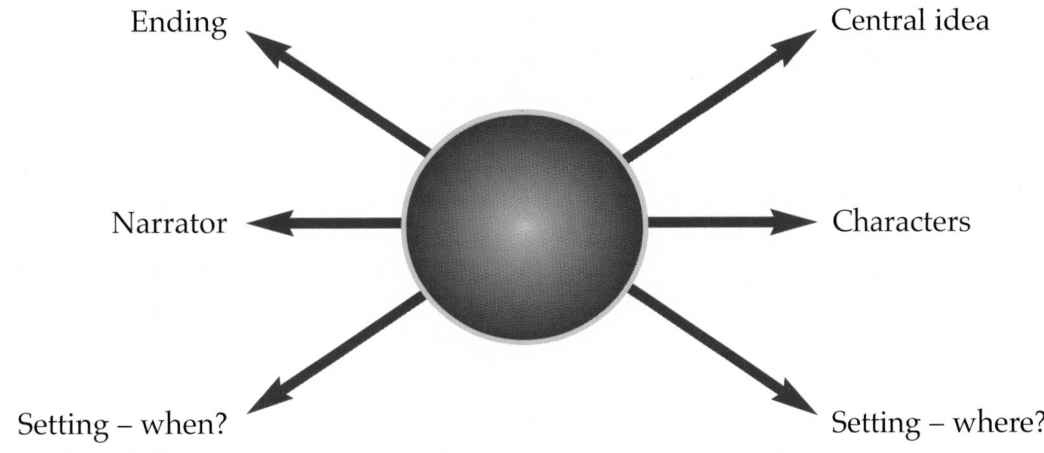

- Plan the sequence of events briefly as a flow diagram.
- Draft your work carefully (you can follow the Drafting Route to help you). With your partner, suggest any changes which might be made to further improve the story before you start writing.
- Write the story on your own.
- When you have finished writing your story, compare it with stories of others in your class.
- Comment on each other's work, using a review sheet like this:

Are the characters interesting and convincing?	
Is the setting described well? Can you imagine it?	
Is the central idea original and intriguing?	
Is the ending unexpected but believable?	
Who is the narrator?	
Could the language give more details or atmosphere?	

- Discuss your answers with the authors of the stories you commented on.

THE END OF *A MESSAGE FROM THE PIG-MAN*

It had gone. Eric peered round, but the light, though faint, was not as faint as that. He could see that the bucket had gone. *The Pig-man had already been.*

Seven–eight–nine–ten, his steps were joyous and light. Back in the house, where it was warm and bright and his train was waiting.

'The Pig-man's gone, Mum. The bucket's not there.'

She frowned, hands deep in the pudding-basin. 'Oh, yes, I do believe I heard him. But it was only a moment ago. Yes, it was just before I called you, darling. It must have been that that made me think of it.'

'Yes?' he said politely, putting down the carrier.

'So if you nip along, dear, you can easily catch him up. And I do want that stuff out of the way.'

'Catch him up?' he asked, standing still in the doorway.

'Yes, dear, *catch him up*.' she answered rather sharply (the Efficient Young Mother knows when to be Firm). 'He can't possibly be more than a very short way down the road.'

Before she had finished Eric was outside the door and running. This was a technique he knew. It was the same as getting into icy cold water. If it was the end, if the Pig-man seized him by the hand and dragged him off to his hut, well, so much the worse. Swinging the paper carrier in his hand, he ran fast through the dusk.

The back view of the Pig-man was much as he had expected it to be. A slow, rather lurching gait, hunched shoulders, and old hat crushed down on his head (to hide his ears?) and the pail in his hand. Plod, plod, as if he were tired. Perhaps this was just a ruse, though, probably he could pounce quickly enough when his wicked little eyes saw a nice tasty little boy or something . . . did the Pig-man eat birds? Or cats?

Eric stopped. He opened his mouth to call to the Pig-man, but the first time he tried, nothing came out except a small rasping squeak. His heart was banging like fireworks going off. He could hardly hear anything.

'Mr Pig-man!' he called, and this time the words came out clear and rather high.

The jogging old figure stopped, turned, and looked at him.

Eric could not see properly from where he stood. But he *had* to see. Everything, even his fear, sank and drowned in the raging tide of his curiosity. He moved forward. With each step he saw more clearly. The Pig-man was just an ordinary old man.

'Hello, sonny. Got some stuff there for the old grunters?'

Eric nodded, mutely, and held out his offering. What old grunters? What did he mean?

The Pig-man put down his bucket. He had ordinary hands, ordinary arms. He took the lid off. Eric held out the paper carrier, and the Pig-man's hand actually touched his own for a second. A flood of gratitude rose up inside him. The Pig-man tipped the scraps into the bucket and handed the carrier back.

'Thanks, sonny,' he said.

'Who's it for?' Eric asked, with another rush of articulateness. His voice seemed to have a life of its own.

The Pig-man straightened up, puzzled. Then he laughed, in a gurgling sort of way, but not like a pig at all.

'Arh aarh Harh Harh,' the Pig-man went. 'Not for me, if that's whatcher mean, arh harh'.

He put the lid back on the bucket. 'It's for the old grunters,' he said. 'The old porkers. Just what they likes. Only not fruit skins. I leave a note, sometimes, about what not to put in. Never fruit skins. It gives 'em the belly-ache'.

He was called the Pig-man because he had some pigs that he looked after.

'Thank-you,' said Eric. 'Goodnight.' He ran back towards the house, hearing the Pig-man, the ordinary old man, the ordinary usual normal old man, say in his just ordinary old man's voice, 'Goodnight, sonny'.

So that was how you did it. You just went straight ahead, not worrying about this or that. Like getting into cold water. You just did it.

He slowed down as he got to the gate. For instance, if there was a question that you wanted to know the answer to, and you had always just felt you couldn't ask, the thing to do was to ask it. Just straight out, like going up to the Pig-man. Difficult things, troubles, questions, you just treated them like the Pig-man.

So that was it!

The warm light shone through the crack of the door. He opened it and went in. His mother was standing at the table, her hands still working the cake mixture about. She would let him scrape out the basin, and the spoon – he would ask for the spoon, too. But not straight away. There was a more important thing first.

He put the paper carrier down and went up to her. 'Mum', he said. 'Why can't Dad be with us even if Donald is here? I mean, why can't he live with us as well as Donald?'

His mother turned and went to the sink. She put the tap on and held her hands under it.

'Darling,' she called.

'Yes?' came Donald's voice.

'D'you know what he's just said?'

'What?'

'He's just asked . . .' She turned the tap off and dried her hands, not looking at Eric. 'He wants to know why we can't have Jack to live with us.'

There was a silence, then Donald said, quietly, so that his voice only just reached Eric's ears, 'That's a hard one.'

'You can scrape out the basin,' his mother said to Eric. She lifted him up and kissed him. Then she rubbed her cheek along leaving a wet smear. 'Poor little Ekky,' she said in a funny voice.

She put him down and he began to scrape out the pudding-basin, certain at least of one thing, that grown-ups were mad and silly and he hated them all, all, all.

WHAT NEXT?

In this unit, you have read extracts from several short stories and discussed them with other members of your group. You have defined common features of short stories and written your own versions.

If you have enjoyed working on short stories, you may wish to develop your skills further:

- Discuss the ending of *A Message from the Pig-Man* with a partner. Do you think it is a good ending? Was it expected? Would you have preferred the story to end differently?
- Try reading some more short stories. (There is a wide range of excellent stories in *Inside Stories 1, 2* and *3* by Peter and Susan Benton, published by Hodder & Stoughton.)
- Compare at least two of the stories you have read, saying which one:
  - has the most intriguing opening
  - makes the best use of language, packing in the most detail
  - successfully maintains the suspense
  - has the most original, surprising but believable ending
- Look at your favourite short story and write about the narrator:
  - Is the narrator a character in the story and, if so, how does the language suggest what the narrator is like?
  - Is the story told in the third person (he, she, they) and, if so, what impressions do you get of each character, and how does the author give these impressions?
- Write a newspaper article about the events in one of the stories you have read – you may want to suggest a possible explanation for any strange events. Include important quotes from key witnesses.

Extract One (page 6) is taken from *A Pair of Silk Stockings* by Kate Chopin.

Extract Two (page 7) is taken from *The Bellows of the Fire* by Rose Tremain.

Extract Three (page 8) is taken from *Through the Tunnel* by Doris Lessing.

Extract Four (page 8) is taken from *Flowers for Algernon* by Daniel Keyes.

UNIT TWO

The Language Factory

In this unit you will concentrate on improving your writing skills by learning to recognise errors in other people's work and produce edited texts for customers of The Language Factory. You will develop your skills as:

SPEAKERS AND LISTENERS

by discussing your work with others
by talking about how to edit texts

READERS

by looking at different styles of reading and analysing how they are used for different purposes
by identifying the characteristics of a good read

WRITERS

by looking carefully at samples of writing and learning how to recognise errors
by producing a selection of edited work for a particular audience

In order to become a language expert employed at The Language Factory you need to start by applying for a job there. Over the page, you will find an advert. As you work through the unit, you will be required to demonstrate that you can work at Beginner, Intermediate and Advanced levels and, if you are good enough, you will get the certificates to prove it.

It's hard work at The Language Factory but, as a fully qualified language expert, you will have no problems knowing what to do when faced with a dissatisfied customer returning a faulty sentence or a struggling writer desperate for the latest in fancy phrases.

The Language Factory

requires

language experts to join the complaints' department. The complaints department works at different levels of expertise. Applicants will have the opportunity to show their skills by working through the levels, Beginner, Intermediate and Advanced.

The ability to work quickly and accurately is very important.

In the information pack that it sent out to everybody who shows an interest in the job, you find a short test which you are asked to fill in so that the Personnel Department at The Language Factory can decide whether or not you are the kind of person the company is looking for. It's a letter which a customer brought in because she knew it wasn't right, but couldn't work out why.

You are asked to proof read the letter and report on the number of errors that it contains. If you can find twenty or more, the company might decide to include you on their fast track training scheme.

Dear Mrs Banks,

john will be stoping school diners from nex monday. he will have a sanwich luch instead like lots the other childrn

Wen he has finshed luch I hope he well not be stoped fom chating to the others. Its very important for him chat and make friends.

Yours sincerely,

(Mrs) Susen smith.

All Trainees working as Language Experts are issued with a Guidance Manual to make sure that they know the standards that are expected of them. Page one of the Manual sets out the requirements at Beginner Level.

BEGINNER LEVEL

To work at Beginner Level you need to be able to edit simple texts. The quality assurance section who check your work will be paying particular attention to the following:

Spelling

You should be able to recognise all simple spelling errors, particularly initial blends, the effect of the 'magic e', and the use of correct vowels.

Punctuation

Recognition of when to use full stops and capital letters is essential. You should also be able to make sensible choices about when it is appropriate to start a new paragraph.

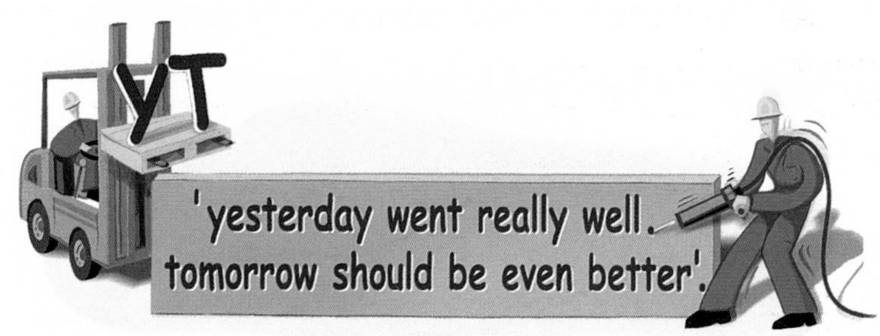

Style

You must be able to recognise that a particular style of writing is needed for different purposes.

Minor Modifications

It is important that you recognise when a piece of writing could be made much clearer simply by making a few changes to the order of the words.

And so to work … the first complaint.

A customer has returned the leaflet below because of the errors in it. Your task is find those errors and correct them. Produce a perfect leaflet. Use the section from the Guidance Manual below to help you.

The South Wests Largest Fun Park

fun Pool

Indoor and Outdoor heated pools with frilling water slides including Crazy River where you shot the rapids in a tyre, and a Kiddies Splash Pool plus a Picnic and sunbathing area. Out 18 hole meadowland 5720 yard, Par and Play for just £15 a round. Why not bring some friends and enjoy a game with a meal and a drink afterwards in the clubhouse

fun Park

50 Discount ticket special

Browse around the garden center. you will be suprised by te variety of plants pots andgarden,camping accessories

Don't forget!

- Sentences begin with capital letters.
- Paragraphs tell you when there is a change in setting or time. You recognise a paragraph when the first line is indented from the margin.
- When trying to spot wrong spellings, ask yourself 'Does it look wright? Does it sound right?'.

A FOUL-UP IN THE FICTION DEPARTMENT

Some of the most highly skilled staff work in the fiction department, where they can use language to do almost anything. But even there, things sometimes go wrong.

A customer has ordered a complete story. The story is a dream come true but some of the words have been put in the wrong order. Can you edit the work so it becomes easier to read?

As I was looking at the paper whilst having breakfast I noticed an Ad. I at it looked closely and saw to my surprise it said 'Like being a spy do you? Well here's your chance to make your dream come true. Apply to Controller, Thornfield Hall, The Square SN12 8ZQ Buckinghamshire' I sent away immediately for details. I had dreamt of being a spy all my life.

I became a nervous wreck waiting for the sound of the letter box in the morning. Twelve days later the letter box with clattered a joyful sound. I was for interview invited.

I up there drove and parked outside. The building was magnificent. The path to the front door had huge trees towering high each side of it.

I knocked on the door which was made of marble. The echo filled the empty atmosphere. A butler opened the door and into the room led me to where the other candidates were. I was given a sheet. It said 'Decode the message' I found that easy. The next test was an examination paper. I was the last one to finish. I was late too I thought. I shivered as the examiner looked at my paper, 'Failed' he said. I was in a trance as I walked back towards my seat with my useless attempt. I'll try again I thought.

This time I read the instruction sheet more carefully and collected paper another. This time I knew I could pass. Almost every answer I knew. I had passed this time. The examiner smiled. I was ready for the next test.

After the day I went home confidently to await another letter. A letter that would make my dream come true and change my life for ever.

CROSSED WIRES

Sometimes problems occur when a department receives delivery of a style that just isn't the right one for the job.

See if you can sort this one out. A customer has ordered several different texts: a newspaper report, a menu, a piece of poetry. Unfortunately, the department has mixed up the order and inappropriate styles have been used. Identify the style of the writing, say what it should have been, and work out what went wrong?

1 Customer: 'Please do me a newspaper report about the fund raising event I am organising …

Reporter: Tell me about the fund raising event.
Organiser: It was very exciting.
Reporter: Who was there?
Organiser: Three local television presenters from the BBC.
Reporter: What was the aim of the evening?
Organiser: To raise money for the local hospice.
Reporter: What sort of activities were going on during the course of the evening?
Organiser: An auction, tombola and a talent show.

CHEF'S SPECIAL CAUSES SENSATION

The starter choice tonight at Foodies, the new town centre gourmet restaurant, is already causing interest. 'It's an experiment', said Pierre Lacoste, the chef at the centre of the controversy. 'In addition to prawn cocktail and paté, I'm adding smoked duck to the menu.'

The second course is likely to give diners an even more difficult choice. Top of the menu is a new chicken dish. The idea came from a night out in Paris, but it is likely to be a while before it takes over from the old favourites, salmon steak or pork fillet with new potatoes.

3 Customer: 'Do you do poetry? I'd like a poetry poster for my living room wall?'

Starters

Frost on the window pane
Crystal constellations

Main course

Icy mornings
Bare branches against the sky
A windswept hillside
Served with choice of pewter skies and autumn leaves

Dessert

A selection of dark evenings topped with cloudless skies and stars as hard as diamonds

Congratulations! You have passed the Beginner's Level and have been awarded your first certificate.

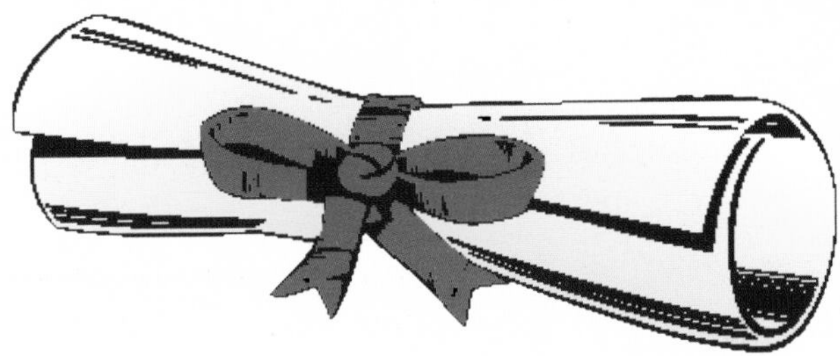

This is to certify that

....

has successfully achieved the

Beginner's Level

at

The Language Factory

and is now eligible to move to the

Intermediate Level

WELL DONE

INTERMEDIATE LEVEL

To work at Intermediate Level you need to be able to edit more complex texts. The quality assurance section who check your work will be paying particular attention to the following:

Summarising and Note Taking

To meet the standard you will need to be able to summarise and record information that you have read or been told. This requires a number of specific skills such as:

Skimming a text at speed in order to get a general impression of what it is about

Scanning particular key words in order to check out the meaning

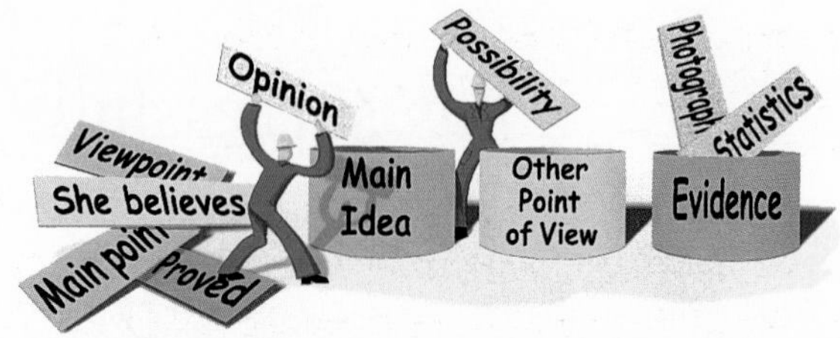

Making notes to record key information and ideas from a text

First and Third Person Narrative

You need to know the difference between first and third person narrative and you need to be able to change a text from first to third person or the other way round.

Dealing with bias

Can you spot when the reader is being manipulated? You need to be able to identify when information has been heavily slanted to give a particular impression.

Changing Tenses

It is important to be sure about the difference between the past, present and future tense. The standard requires you to be aware of the difference and be capable of changing a text from one to the other.

The guidance manual includes a section with practice exercises so that you can try out your skills before actually working on a task for a customer.

BRUSH UP YOUR SKILLS

1 First and Third Person Narrative

- Are the following forms of writing usually written in first or third person narrative? Can you think of any other examples?

diary	science report	history essay
newspaper report	recipe	note to friend
short story	poem	travel brochure

- Rewrite the following passage changing the first person narrator to third person narrator.

'The mountain is near enough,' I said, 'we'll follow the crest,' but I dared not meet Mohamed's eye, nor did I glance at him.

Sometimes one guide led, sometimes the other, and when they flagged, or cast about, I struck ahead. But all at once it was borne in upon me that their resistance and also that of the jungle itself had both given out at the same time. Finding that I was not to be put off they had now cheerfully accepted the position, and put their interest in what lay ahead. As for the jungle, we had left the worst of it behind, and the ridge brought us out into the daylight clear above it. Following one ridge to the next, with occasional drops into the forest, we climbed a straight and broad path which was hemmed in on either side by dense hedges of greenery.

It was paved all the way with the droppings of rhino, buffalo and elephant. I was ahead and walking along with my eyes bent on the spoor, when I came to a grey boulder lying across the path. I was in the act of walking round it when it suddenly heaved itself up beside me with the terrifying snort of a rhino. I recoiled and leapt backwards, while the rhino (who was presumably facing the other way) tore off in the opposite direction. This is only conjecture; for the instant the boulder sprang to life, I did not wait for a second glance but turned and bolted, colliding with the man behind me, who also turned and ran for his life shouting 'Faru! Faru!' (rhino) and in the twinkling of an eye we had scattered like chaff.

2 Dealing with Bias

A well-known travel company has produced travel brochures for specially targeted customers. Look closely at the information they include in their two brochures. Both brochures are selling the same Spanish Island even though the name is spelt differently.

Majorca

Cala D'Or

Cala D'Or is a smart sophisticated resort on the south-east coast, consisting of eight or nine beautiful sandy coves. They are small, popular and can get crowded simply because they are so delightful. The largest, Cala Gran, is forty yards wide and a hundred yards deep.

Hotel Marina

This is a place to relax with an ice-cold drink, while the ACTIV Representative makes sure the kids are having fun in the idyllic cove below.

Location

The Marina faces its sister hotel, the Crete Marina, across the pretty cove of Cala Egos, where calm, blue water laps on gently shelving sand. The two hotels share some facilities, and are just 75m from local shops and bars. There are 37 steps to the beach, which little legs should manage, but wheelchairs won't. You hop on the bus or the mini-train, or catch a taxi into the centre of cosmopolitan Cala d'Or, 2.5km away. Stop off on the way at the marina to take a peek at the yachts. The resort of Cala d'Or has numerous beautiful small sandy coves.

Swimming pool

The charming free-form swimming pool has a children's section, and a little white bridge divides the shallow from the deep end.

The sloping sun terrace leads you straight to the beach, so you can roll out of the pool and into the sea, and there's a pool bar to quench your thirst on the spot.

Sports and activities

Get up off your sunbed, and brush up your tennis or join in the volleyball. There's a cheerful daytime Thomson Superfamily activities programme, featuring games in and around the pool, including Family Splash, Giant Jenga, Giant Connect Four, skittles and lots more.

Entertainment

This superior package includes Thomson Entertainers leading daytime and evening shows and 3 professional shows each week – so sit back and enjoy. The fun-filled evening shows and professional acts take place outside in high season, so there's no going to bed early if your room faces the pool. Entertainment is shared with guests in the Crete Marina.

Meals

Children have their own buffet, where choices like spaghetti bolognese and jelly and ice cream bring squeals of delight. Parents look forward to peaceful – romantic even! – conversation over the weekly Gala dinner, while we supervise the kids.

Prices are based on half board for two adults sharing a room with 2 or 3 beds, bath, wc and balcony. Double rooms can take 2 adults and 2 children (on camp and sofa beds), but maybe cramped when fully occupied. Larger family rooms taking up to 4 adults and a cot, interconnecting rooms and rooms with seaview are also available to book, and cannot be requested if unavailable. For interconnecting rooms request two TW3CON rooms. All rooms have childproof locks on balcony doors. Towels are changed daily and linen twice weekly.

Mallorca

Cala d'Or

On the south east coast of Mallorca, Cala d'Or is a stylish resort much favoured for sailing, with a bustling marina and one of the most exclusive yacht clubs on the island.

HOTEL ASTORIA

A beachside hotel with breathtaking seaviews, the Astoria is for those in search of peace and tranquillity in a relaxed yet elegant setting. The hotel lobby with its pillars and domed ceilings gives the impression of an exclusive private villa. On the whole, this is a quiet hotel with lazy days passed by the pool or on the beach and tranquil nights spent enjoying a drink in the bar. The centre of Cala d'Or is a 200 metre walk away. The hotel is not suitable for the less mobile due to the number of steps.

"ideal for a lazy and relaxing holiday, just enjoying the beach and admiring the views"

- What assumptions have the travel company made about their customers? Use the following headings to help you compare the two brochures:

  language used
  information given
  images used
  page layout

- As a test exercise, try producing a page for each of the above travel agents promoting a leisure centre or hotel near you. Remember that different customers will be looking for different things.

You should be capable now of working at Intermediate Level on real assignments that have been sent to the factory. The one below will test you to the limit.

The following task requires you to employ all the skills that are expected at intermediate level. Read the letters and notes carefully before drawing up the two reports for your supervisor.

'Please provide an exciting, well written report for inclusion in local paper. Report must be in third person and in the past tense (except for quotations). Unsure of bias required by customer so you are to produce two reports, one in favour of the shop and one against. Facts must remain the same as in notes. To be handed to me for checking'.

The Supervisor,
The Language Factory,

Dear Sir or Madam,

I have just started a new job as a journalist and have been asked to produce a report on the opening of a new store. As you can see my notes are in a mess and I need help. I would be grateful if you could provide me with a 200 word report.

Yours anxiously,

Rovingree Porter

Rovingree Porter

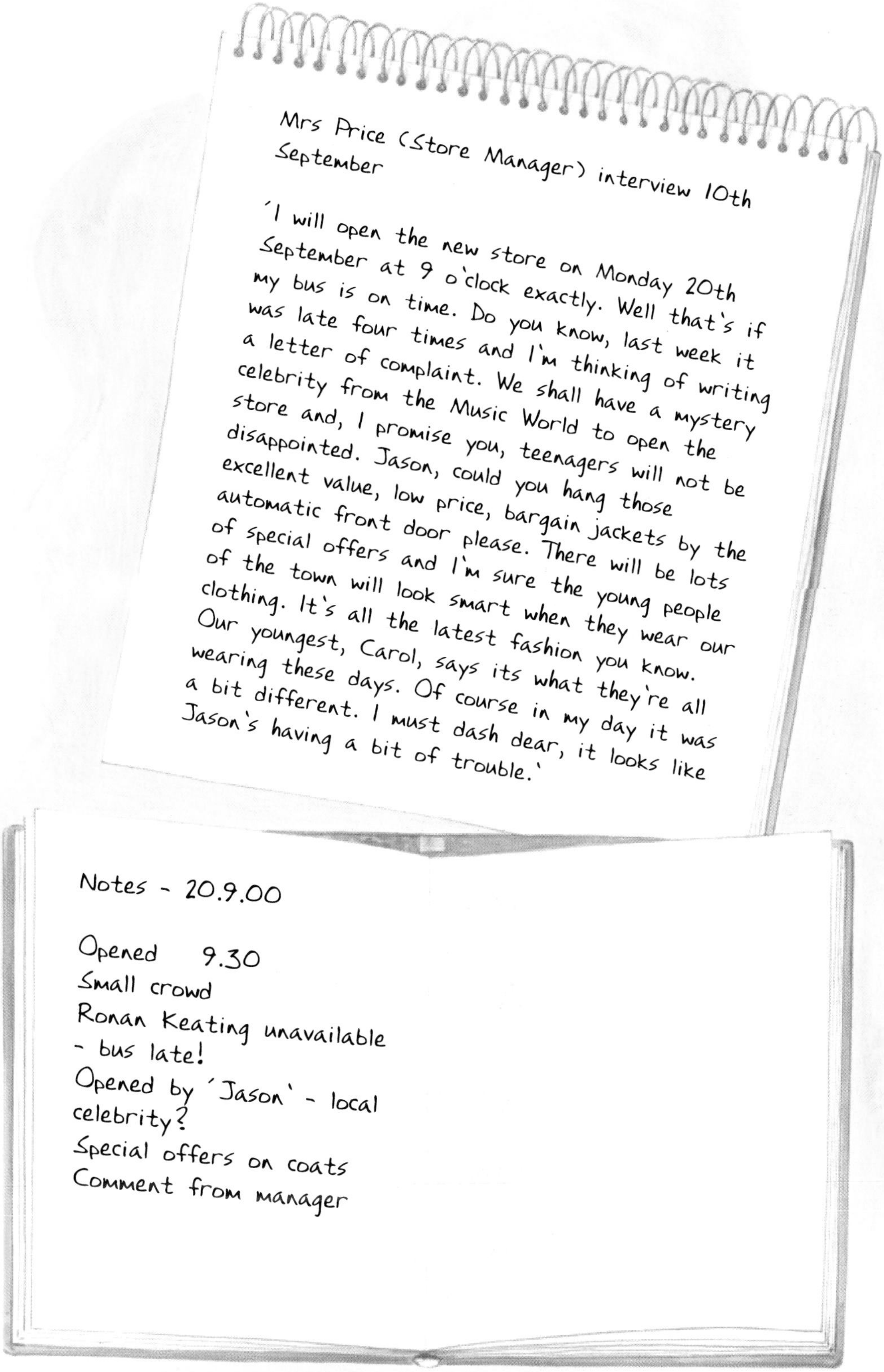

Mrs Price (Store Manager) interview 10th September

'I will open the new store on Monday 20th September at 9 o'clock exactly. Well that's if my bus is on time. Do you know, last week it was late four times and I'm thinking of writing a letter of complaint. We shall have a mystery celebrity from the Music World to open the store and, I promise you, teenagers will not be disappointed. Jason, could you hang those excellent value, low price, bargain jackets by the automatic front door please. There will be lots of special offers and I'm sure the young people of the town will look smart when they wear our clothing. It's all the latest fashion you know. Our youngest, Carol, says its what they're all wearing these days. Of course in my day it was a bit different. I must dash dear, it looks like Jason's having a bit of trouble.'

Notes - 20.9.00

Opened 9.30
Small crowd
Ronan Keating unavailable
- bus late!
Opened by 'Jason' - local
celebrity?
Special offers on coats
Comment from manager

LANGUAGE FACTORY LANGUAGE FACTORY

This is to certify that

....

has successfully achieved the

Intermediate

Level

at

The Language Factory

and is now eligible to move to the

Advanced

Level

WELL DONE

LANGUAGE FACTORY LANGUAGE FACTORY

ADVANCED LEVEL

To work at Advanced Level you need to be able to recognise, appreciate and produce different genres of writing. The word 'genre' refers to the different categories or types of writing there are. Only the most experienced and skilled workers are permitted to work in the Genre Department. You should read and work through your Guidance Manual carefully to ensure that you are ready to tackle tasks at this level.

- All writing can be organised into different genres. Below are some examples. Can you add any more?

- We recognise genres from the style of writing. Can you identify the genres of the following extracts?

I was quite happy in my new place, and if there was one thing that I missed, it must not be thought that I was discontented; all who had to do with me were good, and I had a light airy stable and the best of food. What more could I want? Why, liberty! For three years and a half of my life I had had all the liberty I could wish for; but now, week after week, month after month, and no doubt year after year, I must stand up in a stable night and day except when I am wanted, and then I must be just as steady and quiet as any old horse who has worked twenty years.

As soon as he stepped into the hall, Andrew knew at once that something was wrong. He couldn't tell what it was; he was simply aware of a dark wave of dread that rose to meet him the minute the front door was opened.

'Ah, there you are,' the woman said. 'You must be Andrew,. We were wondering where you'd got to. I'm Carol Sharman.'

Andrew blinked at her, dazzled by the light in the hall. He wanted to turn and run, he wanted to get away from the house, but he couldn't. He had to stay.

There was once upon a time a good man who had two children: a girl by a first wife, and a boy by the second. The girl was a white as milk, and her lips were like cherries. Her hair was like golden silk, and it hung to the ground. Her brother loved her dearly, but her wicked stepmother hated her. 'Child,' said the stepmother one day, 'go to the grocer's shop and buy me a pound of candles.' She gave her the money; and the little girl went, brought the candles, and started on her return.

'What is it, then – a fire?'

'No; a client. It seems that a young lady has arrived in a considerable state of excitement, who insists upon seeing me. She is waiting now in the sitting-room. Now, when young ladies wander about the metropolis at this hour of the morning, and knock sleepy people out of their beds, I presume that it is something very pressing which they have to communicate. Should it prove to be an interesting case, you would, I am sure, wish to follow it from the outset. I thought, at any rate, that I should call you and give you the chance.'

Most grandmothers are lovely, kind, helpful old ladies, but not this one. She spent all day and every day sitting in her chair by the window, and she was always complaining, grousing, grouching, grumbling, griping about something or other. Never once, even on her best days, had she smiled at George and said, 'Well, how are you this morning, George?' or 'Why don't you and I have a game of Snakes and Ladders?' or 'How was school today?' She didn't seem to care about other people, only about herself. She was a miserable old grouch.

1 Letters

Our clients often require help in writing and replying to letters. Here are a selection of requests we have received. Produce the letters they should write making sure the layout of each letter is correct.

PLEASE MRS BUTLER

Please Mrs Butler
This boy Derek Drew
Keeps copying my work, Miss.
What shall I do?

Go and sit in the hall, dear.
Go and sit in the sink.
Take your books on the roof, my lamb.
Do whatever you think.

Please Mrs Butler
This boy Derek Drew
Keeps taking my rubber, Miss.
What shall I do?

Keep it in your hand, dear.
Hide it up your vest.
Swallow it if you like, my love.
Do what you think best.

Please Mrs Butler
This boy Derek Drew
Keeps calling me rude names, Miss.
What shall I do?

Lock yourself in the cupboard, dear.
Run away to sea.
Do whatever you can, my flower.
But don't ask me!

Allan Ahlberg

After due consideration I feel I should write home to the parents of Derek Drew. What advice should I give?

Mrs Butler

MALCOLM

Miserable Malcolm from Morcambe
had Rottweilers but would not walk 'em.
They were stuck in all day
but no muck would they lay
because Malcambe had managed to
cork 'em.

John Hegley

We have recently received a complaint about the treatment of these dogs and wish to write a very stern letter outlining how the owner should be caring for these animals and what action we shall take if the situation does not change immediately.

RSPCA

SURVIVOR

Everyday,
I think about dying.
About disease, starvation,
violence, terrorism, war,
the end of the world.

It helps
keep my mind off things.

Roger McGough

I am very worried about my friend's mental health and the horrid thoughts he dwells on. How can I persuade him that there are wonderful things happening in the world and help achieve a healthier outlook on life?

A friend

2 A Guide Book for Travellers

The tourist industry in Transylvania has been boosted considerably by Bram Stoker's frightening book *Dracula*. Many people believe in the myth of Dracula and now want to travel to Transylvania to investigate the mystery for themselves.

- The Transylvania Tourist Board wish to update their holiday guide. Use the information below to produce a useful and informative guide for would-be vampire hunters. Carry out your own research and add any other interesting facts.

DRACULA'S HOMELAND

Vlad Dracula
Bram Stoker gave his character Dracula a real ancestor – Vlad Dracula (c.1431-76), prince of Wallachia, an ancient kingdom now part of Romania.

Son of Dracul
Vlad's father was Vlad Dracul, meaning "devil" or "dragon". His son become known as Dracula, or "son of Dracul".

Transylvania
Today Transylvania is a province of Romania. When Dracula was written, the region was part of Austro-Hungary.

The landscape
Jonathan Harker saw a land of unspoilt beauty dotted with towns and villages remaining unchanged for centuries.

The people
Transylvania was a land of many peoples, including Magyars (from Hungary), Romanians, Szekelys, Slovaks, and gypsies. Out of this rich cultural mix grew a range of superstitions about vampires.

Gypsy culture
When gypsies settled in eastern Europe in the 1400s, they brought with them their vampire beliefs. The gypsies' name for vampire is *mullo.*

Klausenburgh
Jonathan Harker travelled here by train from Budapest in Austro-Hungry. Klausenburgh was the great capital of Transylvania, and its many fine buildings are Hungarian in style. Today it is known by the Romanian name of Cluj.

Bistritz
It was in Bistritz, today called Bistrita, that Harker was first warned about the dangers of vampires. There is a hotel in Bistrita called the *Coroana de aur* ("Golden Krone") after the inn where Harker stayed.

Borgo Pass
The Borgo Pass is one of the most dramatic settings in the novel. Set high up in the Carpathian Mountains, the Pass and the surrounding area are breathtaking, with sheer mountain faces and forests of fir trees.

Dracula's Castle
Dracula's home may have been based on a real castle in Romania. Various sites have been suggested:

1 Bran Castle, built in the 13th century. Vlad the Impaler was both a guest and later a prisoner here. Its dark rooms and corridors tie in with Bram Stoker's description.

2 The 13th-century castle at Hunadoara, where Vlad Dracul is believed to have been a guest.

3 The castle north of Curtea de Arges that Vlad the Impaler-built and lived in.

THE BOOK AND THE LEGEND

Beliefs vary, but generally a vampire is a dead human who returns from the grave and sucks the blood of the living. Vampire myths are rooted in the idea of blood as the source of life, and that drinking it would renew strength. Bram Stoker got many of his ideas about vampires by reading about the legends of eastern Europe. But he also added some of his own ideas and brought the vampire legend up to date.

What do vampires look like?
Many vampires from eastern Europe folklore had a deathly-pale complexion like that of a corpse, and had a strong smell of death. Transylvanian vampires had foul breath and were horribly ugly, with hypnotic blood-red eyes. In the novel, Dracula has pale skin and long fingernails. His eyes flashed red when he was angry. His very red lips covered long pointed teeth.

The history of vampires
Vampire stories can be traced back to ancient civilizations. The earliest known picture of a blood-sucking human appears on a Babylonian cylinder seal, about 4,000 years old. In India, tales were written about a vampire who hangs upside-down in a tree, like a bat. Vampires also appear in the legends of ancient Egypt, China, Rome, and Greece.

Vampires in eastern Europe

In the 16th and 17th centuries, vampire legends developed throughout eastern Europe. In Hungary, a countess called Elizabeth Bathory was accused of torturing and murdering young women. It was said she bit her victims' flesh and drank their blood.

Transylvania
Vampire folklore flourished in the remote mountainous land of Transylvania, with its rich mix of ethnic groups and traditions. Here people believed that you would become a vampire if you were born with teeth, or if you were the seventh son of a seventh son.

If you have successfully undertaken all of the work suggested in the 'Brush up Your Skills' section of the Guidance Manual, you will be ready to take on some of the work that is piling up in the Genre Department.

SUIT YOU SIR!

The Genre Department has received the following request from NASA (North American Space Agency). Read the memo and then complete the job as requested. Use the article below to give you some ideas if you need them.

Memo

NASA are having a stock clearance and wish to sell off their surplus supply of space suits. Please prepare an eye-catching, informative advertisement targeted at space cadets. NASA has provided the attached information sheet for your use.

SPACE SUITS AND SPACE WALKS

When astronauts leave the safety of the spacecraft, they have to wear space suits to stay alive. A space suit is like a mini-spacecraft, supplying air and protection from dangerous radiation and speeding dust. It also presses down on the body – just as the atmosphere on Earth does – to stop air from bubbling out of the bloodstream, which would be fatal.

A space suit has to be very bulky to keep out the cold of space and the heat of the Sun, so there are tucks and folds in the layers of material to make it easier for the astronauts to move their arms and legs. Underneath the space suit, next to the skin, there is a cooling suit with small tubes carrying water to take away body heat. The helmet has a dark visor to protect the eyes from ultraviolet light from the Sun, and earphones and a microphone for talking to other astronauts. The backpack carries supplies of both air and water.

Sealed inside their suits, astronauts can work in space for several hours, tied to the spacecraft to stop them from floating away. To go further from their spacecraft, space-shuttle astronauts wear a Manned Manoeuvring Unit (or MMU) on their back. This has little jets to move or turn them in any direction. They can even go out and capture a satellite, then bring it back to the shuttle for repairs.

Your next task in the Genre Department is outlined in the memo below.

URGENT

Memo: To Advanced Skills Workers

We have just received the attached fax from a customer. Things have gone seriously wrong! You must use all your skills to put this right immediately. The reputation of the company is in your hands.

Fax

As you know, I am building my career as a television writer and novelist and I have been asked to submit a selection of pieces for consideration by a huge media company. I sent all my work to you for editing and YOU HAVE LOST IT!!! My deadline is approaching fast and I must have these written pieces. My work must be replaced with top quality, well-presented work or else!!!

Missing work to be replaced

- A holiday guide for 'Out of this World Destinations'
- A script for the first episode of a new TV soap set on a space station
- The opening page of my latest science fiction novel
- An advertisement for pre-packed, nutritious space meals in tablet form
- A news report on the opening of a new luxury space hotel

Please enclose a letter of apology with replacement work.

WHAT'S NEXT?

In this unit you have looked at what makes a good piece of writing, practised your proof reading skills and widened your knowledge of different genres. When you have finished all the tasks, you may wish to have a go at producing the following.

- Develop your own manual of the skills needed to work in a Language Factory
- Produce a promotional video on the skills needed to work in a Language Factory
- Develop your own website advertising the service a Language Factory can provide
- Design a leaflet for prospective customers encouraging them to use your services as an advanced level Language Expert.

LANGUAGE FACTORY LANGUAGE FACTORY

This is to certify that

....

has successfully achieved the

Advanced

Level

at

The Language Factory

and is now a

qualified language expert

WELL DONE

LANGUAGE FACTORY LANGUAGE FACTORY

UNIT THREE

A Vein of Poetry

'A vein of poetry exists in the hearts of all men.'
Thomas Carlyle

In this unit you will explore several forms of poetry and discover how they work and what makes them appealing. You will develop your skills as:

SPEAKERS AND LISTENERS

by exploring the sounds of words and word patterns in poetry
by listening to the rhythms of poems and creating your own

READERS

by reading different styles of poems
by looking at how poets stimulate your imagination

WRITERS

by becoming a poet, drafting and writing a range of poems
by keeping a poetry journal

Robert Burns

When you turn this page, you will read a poem which is familiar to you. Think about where you have heard it before...

AULD LANG SYNE

by Robert Burns

SHOULD auld acquaintance be forgot,
And never brought to min'?
Should auld acquaintance be forgot,
And auld lang syne?

For auld lang syne, my dear.
For auld lang syne,
We'll tak a cup o' kindness yet,
For auld lang syne.

auld lang syne – *old long ago*

Poetry is a way of communicating thoughts and feelings. The poet uses words and rhythms to create pictures in the mind of the reader or listener. You may have already learned something about writing descriptions to help tell a story. A storyteller can take time to explain details, whereas a poet often needs to make sure that all the details are in a short description. For this reason, the poet chooses the most appropriate form for his or her poem.

In this unit, you will look at some different forms of poetry, some to be read and some to be spoken.

'AULD LANG SYNE'

Read again the two verses of this poem.

- In a small group, discuss when, where, how and why you hear versions of 'Auld Lang Syne'.
- What do the speakers of 'Auld Lang Syne' usually do with the rhythm?
- Most people find these verses easy to remember. Discuss why you think this is.
- What emotions does 'Auld Lang Syne' stir up?

'Auld Lang Syne' is a poem which uses the form of a traditional ballad. A ballad is one of the oldest types of poetry. Originally, ballads were passed on by word of mouth. Then, minstrels travelled around the country and told and sang ballads at fairs, in courtyards, wherever people gathered, much like a storyteller with his tales. 'Ballare' in Latin meant 'to dance', and 'balade' in Old French meant 'dancing-song'. We use the term 'ballad' for a song or a poem which tells a story.

HELP

Ballad – a song or poem telling a story in short, rhyming verses.

A traditional ballad, like a traditional folk tale, uses certain patterns so that it is easy to remember. You will find that ballads usually have short verses which rhyme (often the second and fourth lines, but not always). They may also contain repeated lines.

In 1797, the poet Samuel Taylor Coleridge wrote a ballad about an old sailor who tells an unwilling listener how his ship was caught in a storm. When the sailor, or 'mariner' as he is called in the poem, 'holds him with his glittering eye', the listener is mesmerised: he 'listens like a three years' child'...

READING THE BALLAD

- You now know that ballads were traditionally sung. Therefore, it is a good idea to read the next ballad aloud, sharing the verses among your group.

1 First, turn to 'The Rime of the Ancient Mariner' on pages 58–59 and read the notes to the left of the verses. These will help you to understand what is happening, and so make your first reading more successful.

2 Read all of the verses to yourself and then discuss what the poem is about with your group. You can then organise who will read which verses.

3 Read the poem aloud. Do not read fast – you need to give your audience time to take in what is happening.

An extract from

THE RIME OF THE ANCIENT MARINER

by Samuel Taylor Coleridge

PART 1

An ancient Mariner meeteth three Gallants bidden to a wedding-feast, and detaineth one.

It is an ancient Mariner,
And he stoppeth one of three.
'By thy long grey beard and glittering eye,
Now wherefore stopp'st thou me?

The Bridegroom's doors are opened wide,
And I am next of kin;
The guests are met, the feast is set:
May'st hear the merry din.'

The Wedding Guest is spell-bound by the eye of the old seafaring man, and constrained to hear his tale.

He holds him with his skinny hand,
'There was a ship,' quoth he.
'Hold off! unhand me, grey-beard loon!'
Eftsoons his hand dropt he.

He holds him with his glittering eye –
The Wedding-Guest stood still,
And listens like a three years' child:
The Mariner hath his will.

The Wedding-Guest sat on a stone:
He cannot choose but hear;
And thus spake on that ancient man,
The bright-eyed Mariner.

The Mariner tells how the ship sailed southward with a good wind and fair weather, till it reached the line.

'The ship was cheered, the harbour cleared,
Merrily did we drop
Below the kirk, below the hill,
Below the lighthouse top.

The Sun came up upon the left,
Out of the sea came he!
And he shone bright, and on the right
Went down into the sea.

Higher and higher every day,
Till over the mast at noon –'
The Wedding-Guest here beat his breast,
For he heard the loud bassoon.

The Wedding-Guest heareth the bridal music; but the Mariner continueth his tale.

The bride hath paced into the hall,
Red as a rose is she;
Nodding their heads before her goes
The merry minstrelsy.

The Wedding-Guest he beat his breast,
Yet he cannot choose but hear;
And thus spake on that ancient man,
The bright-eyed Mariner.

The ship driven by a storm toward the south pole.

'And now the STORM-BLAST came, and he
Was tyrannous and strong:
He struck with his o'ertaking wings,
And chased us south along.

With sloping masts and dipping prow,
As who pursued with yell and blow
Still treads the shadow of his foe,
And forward bends his head,
The ship drove fast, loud roared the blast,
And southward aye we fled.

And now there came both mist and snow,
And it grew wondrous cold:
And ice, mast-high, came floating by,
As green as emerald.

The land of ice, and of fearful sounds where no living thing was to be seen.

And through the drifts the snowy clifts
Did send a dismal sheen:
Nor shapes of men nor beasts we ken –
The ice was all between.

The ice was here, the ice was there,
The ice was all around:
It cracked and growled, and roared and howled,
Like noises in a swound!

Till a great sea-bird, called the Albatross, came through the snow-fog, and was received with great joy and hospitality.

At length did cross an Albatross,
Thorough the fog it came;
As if it had been a Christian soul,
We hailed it in God's name.

It ate the food it ne'er had eat,
And round and round it flew.
The ice did split with a thunder-fit;
The helmsman steered us through!

And lo! The Albatross proveth a bird of good omen, and followeth the ship as it returned northward through fog and floating ice.

And a good south wind sprung up behind;
The Albatross did follow,
And every day, for food or play,
Came to the mariners' hollo!

In mist or cloud, on mast or shroud,
It perched for vespers nine;
Whiles all the night, through fog-smoke white,
Glimmered the white Moon-shine.'

The ancient Mariner inhospitably killeth the pious bird of good omen.

'God save thee, ancient Mariner!
From the fiends, that plague thee thus! –
Why look'st thou so?' – With my cross-bow
I shot the ALBATROSS.

POETRY JOURNAL

- Start to write a Poetry Journal. Write down your first reactions to the poem you have just read. What could you see or hear? What thoughts and feelings did you have? Have you any questions about the poem? What ideas might the writer want to get across?
- Keep adding your thoughts in the journal as you work through this poetry unit. Always date each entry you make. You can write favourite poems, or lines from a poem, in your journal. You can also add illustrations. (Do not wait to be told to write in your journal. You can write in it whenever you want to.)

THE BALLAD, 'THE RIME OF THE ANCIENT MARINER'

- What does the title of the poem tell you?
- In what ways is this a typical ballad? Using your knowledge about ballads, discuss this in your group.
- Read stanzas 11 and 12 again. Coleridge compared the 'storm blast' with a creature. Which type of creature do you think he is comparing the storm with? Why do you think this? Think about all of the elements of a storm and your feelings when you see a storm. Write down the ways in which the creature compares with this.
- In stanza 4, the 'Wedding-Guest stood still, And listens like a three years' child'. Write a brief description of what Coleridge means.

When a poet or writer compares someone or something to something else, using the words 'like' or 'as', we call this a 'simile'. For example, 'John's face turned as red as a beetroot', 'Meeta slept like a baby'.

When a poet or writer makes a comparison by suggesting that someone or something ***is*** something else, such as when Coleridge describes the storm as a creature, we call the description a 'metaphor'. The poet wants you to think about what the two things have in common.

HELP

Simile – a comparison using 'like' or 'as'.
Metaphor – a description of something as something else which has similar features.

You will come across these terms again later in this unit.

PICTURES IN POETRY

The artist, Gustav Doré, was so inspired by Coleridge's use of language that he drew a set of illustrations to accompany the poem.

- Which of the lines from the poem fits Doré's illustration shown here?
- Choose a verse or two of the poem and draw your own illustration. Write the lines that inspired you underneath your drawing.

WRITING A BALLAD

- Before you go on to write your own ballad, look at the rhythm of 'The Rime of the Ancient Mariner'. Read stanzas 2 and 3 aloud and clap the beats as you read. When you write your ballad, check that you keep to a regular rhythm.
- Working in a small group, write your own ballad. You can base it on a story you already know, or a traditional folk-tale. Try to:
  - make a plan of the story you want to tell. Sort out the order of events
  - write it in stanzas of four lines
  - make the second and fourth lines rhyme
  - include exciting, dramatic action
  - include some dialogue (speeches of characters), set out in speech marks
  - use a simile or metaphor
- Read the opening stanzas of four famous ballads which are printed on these pages. They may help you as you write your own.
- You might like to illustrate your poem.
- Record your experience of writing a ballad in your poetry journal. Say how you decided what to write about and how you found your rhymes.

The post-boy drove with fierce career,
For threatening clouds the moon had drowned;
When, as we hurried on, my ear
Was smitten with a startling sound

As if the wind blew many ways,
I heard the sound – and more and more;
It seemed to follow with the chaise,
And still I heard it as before.

From 'Alice Fell; or, Poverty' by William Wordsworth

Three gipsies stood at the Castle gate,
They sang so high, they sang so low;
The lady sate in her chamber late,
Her heart it melted away as snow.

They sang so sweet, they sang so shrill,
That fast her tears began to flow.
And she laid down her silken gown,
Her golden rings, and all her show.

From 'The Wraggle Taggle Gipsies', anon.

'O what can ail thee, knight-at-arms,
Alone and palely loitering?
The sedge has withered from the lake,
And no birds sing.

'O what can ail thee, knight-at-arms,
So haggard and so woe-begone?
The squirrel's granary is full,
And the harvest's done.

From 'La Belle Dame Sans Merci' by John Keats

No stir in the air, no stir in the sea,
The ship was still as she could be,
Her sails from heaven received no motion,
Her keel was steady in the ocean.

Without either sign or sound of their shock
The waves flowed over the Inchcape Rock;
So little they rose, so little they fell,
They did not move the Inchcape Bell.

From 'The Inchcape Rock' by Robert Southey

SONGS

Like ballads, most songs have simple rhythm and rhyme patterns. This is because they were originally set to music.

For example, William Shakespeare included songs in many of his plays. These songs could have several purposes. They:

- entertained a possible rowdy audience in Shakespeare's time
- create atmosphere
- fit the personality of the singer and so help the audience to understand the character
- help to build up a theme in the play
- break the tension of the main plot or even build up the tension

DRUNKEN SONG

Read the song sung in Shakespeare's play, *The Tempest*, by Stefano, the drunken butler who has just survived a terrible sea-storm.

The master, the swabber, the boatswain and I,
The gunner and his mate
Loved Mall, Meg and Marian and Margery,
But none of us cared for Kate;
For she had a tongue with a tang,
Would cry to a sailor, Go hang!
She loved not the savour of tar nor of pitch,
Yet a tailor might scratch her where'er she did itch:
Then to sea, boys, and let her go hang!

The Tempest, Act 2, Scene 2, lines 45-54

- Talk about how you think Stefano might sing this song.
- What impression does this song give you of his character?
- Someone from your group could say or sing the song in the way you think it should be performed.
- How might an audience respond to this song?

OPHELIA'S SONG

In Shakespeare's most famous tragedy, *Hamlet,* Ophelia sings the following song. Ophelia is a gentle young woman. She loves Hamlet but he kills her father. Ophelia goes mad.

And will he not come again?
And will he not come again?
No, no, he is dead:
Go to thy death-bed:
He never will come again.
His beard was as white as snow,
All flaxen was his poll:
He is gone, he is gone.
And we cast away moan:
God ha' mercy on his soul!

Hamlet, Act 4, Scene 5, lines 190–199

- Why do you think Shakespeare chose to have Ophelia singing this song? Discuss this in your group.
- What effects would the song have on the audience? Look back to the suggested purposes and think about what you already know about songs.

The songs you have just read are sung on stage during the plays. Some poets use the song form because of its simplicity, not necessarily to show that it must be performed.

The poet and artist William Blake wrote a whole series of poems which he collected together and called *Songs of Innocence and Experience.* A poem in the 'Songs of Innocence' section often has a 'partner' poem in the 'Songs of Experience' section.

SONGS OF INNOCENCE AND EXPERIENCE

- Read these two songs and write about your first impressions of them in your journal. Which would be a Song of Innocence? Which would be a Song of Experience? Why?

THE TYGER

Tyger! Tyger! burning bright
In the forests of the night;
What immortal hand or eye
Could frame thy fearful symmetry?

In what distant deeps or skies
Burnt the fire of thine eyes?
On what wings dare he aspire?
What the hand dare sieze the fire?

And what shoulder, and what art
Could twist the sinews of thy heart?
And when thy heart began to beat,
What dread hand? and what dread feet?

What the hammer? what the chain,
In what furnace was thy brain?
What the anvil? what dread grasp
Dare its deadly terrors clasp?

When the stars threw down their spears,
And water'd heaven with their tears,
Did he smile his work to see?
Did he who made the Lamb make thee?

Tyger! Tyger! burning bright
In the forests of the night,
What immortal hand or eye
Dare frame thy fearful symmetry?

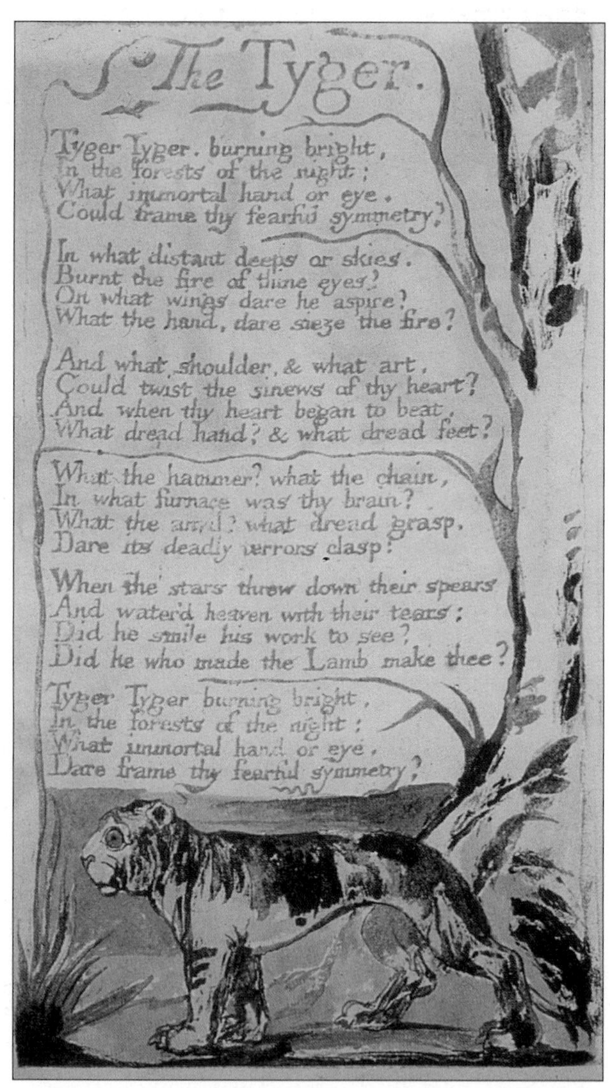

- What questions does Blake ask in these poems?
- Why do you think that Blake asks so many questions? Who might answer them?
- Can you find a line in 'The Tyger' which reminds you of the other poem?

THE LAMB

Little Lamb, who made thee?
Dost thou know who made thee?
Gave thee life, and bid thee feed,
By the stream and o'er the mead;
Gave thee clothing of delight,
Softest clothing, woolly, bright;
Gave thee such a tender voice,
Making all the vales rejoice?
Little Lamb, who made thee?
Dost thou know who made thee?

Little Lamb, I'll tell thee,
Little Lamb, I'll tell thee:
He is callèd by thy name,
For He calls himself a Lamb:
He is meek, and he is mild,
He became a little child.
I a child, and thou a lamb,
We are callèd by His name.
Little Lamb, God bless thee!
Little Lamb, God bless thee!

SONG

by Christina Rossetti

When I am dead, my dearest,
Sing no sad songs for me;
Plant thou no roses at my head,
Nor shady cypress tree:
Be the green grass above me
With showers and dewdrops wet:
And if thou wilt, remember,
And if thou wilt, forget.

I shall not see the shadows,
I shall not feel the rain:
I shall not hear the nightingale
Sing on, as if in pain:
And dreaming through the twilight
That doth not rise nor set,
Haply I may remember,
And haply may forget.

WHEN I AM DEAD, MY DEAREST

- Who do you think the speaker in the poem might be talking to?
- How does the speaker feel about dying?
- Why do you think Christina Rossetti chose to call this poem 'Song' and why did she write it in the form of a song? Discuss this in your group. Do you think that it is meant to be sung?

The skill of the poet lies largely in the ability to make short phrases give the fullest descriptions possible. You looked at the way in which Coleridge describes every aspect of a storm in a few lines. Blake makes us imagine a contrast in colours while giving a sense of power in just the first two lines of 'The Tyger'. You will now go on to look at a form of poetry in which the poet must express everything in only three lines.

HAIKU

A haiku is a type of poem which originally came from Japan. A traditional haiku has three lines with

- five syllables (beats) in the first line
- seven syllables in the second line
- five syllables in the third line = seventeen syllables

Because there are only three short lines in a haiku, every word must be *very* carefully chosen. A haiku does not usually rhyme and it does not need to be read aloud – it is a poem to make you think.

HELP

Syllable – a syllable is part of a word equal to one beat. For example, 'cup' has one syllable, 'hello' has two syllables, 'animal' has three syllables, 'definitely' has four syllables.

HAIKU

Poem in three lines:
five syllables, then seven,
five again; no rhyme.

by Eric Finney

Animal mountains
Sleeping in each other's shade
In Connemara

by Kit Wright

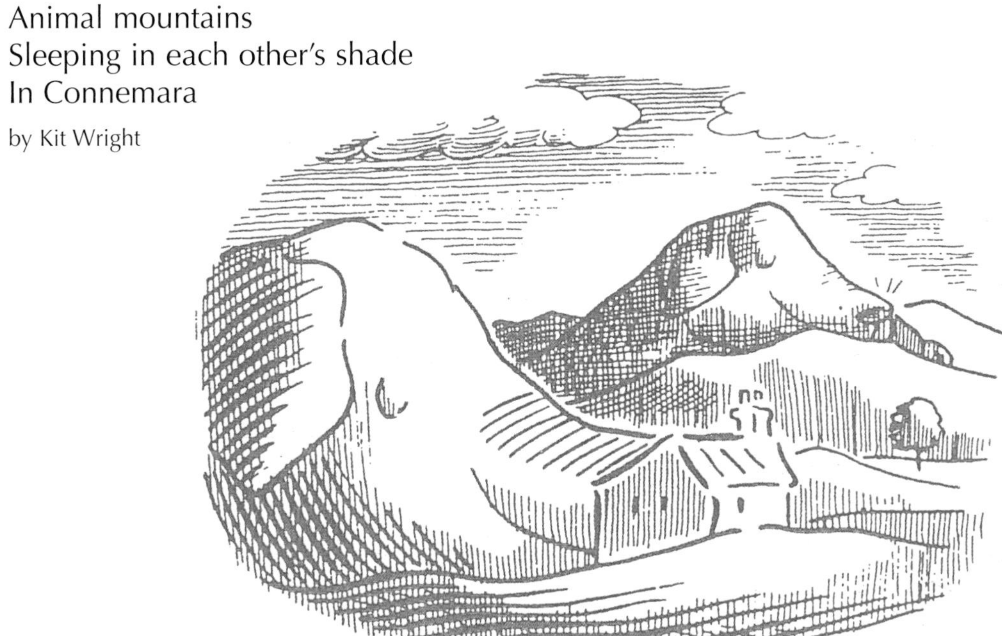

Wolf

1 2 3 4 5
still | on | his | lone | rock

1 2 3 4 5 6 7
stares | at | the | un | caged | stars | and

1 2 3 4 5
cries | in | to | the | night

by Judith Nicholls

TWO HAIKUS

- Read the two haikus.
- Look at 'Wolf'. Discuss with a partner how this poem makes you feel. Think about what you know about wolves. Why are the first words of each line important? There are only two adjectives in the poem but they are carefully chosen to give important information about the wolf – what do they tell us? What does the word 'night' suggest?
- Choose a title for Kit Wright's haiku. Why do you think the poet chose to use the word 'animal' instead of using a particular kind of animal? What does 'in each other's shade' tell us about the mountains?

Some poets choose to write haikus as a series. A series of linked haikus is called a 'renga'.

White water

White water. Canoes
Flip, frail as winter twigs, down
to black river calm.

Across still water
Voices, light laughter, singing
Drift like distant dreams.

Heavy heron flies
Head-tucked, slow winged, sleep-grey, calm.
Lands, and turns to stone.

Did you see the moon
Stealthy as foxes, slip down
To the forest clouds?

by Berlie Doherty

WHITE WATER

- In groups, read through this poem. Spend a few minutes writing about your first responses in your journal.
- Pick out some of the examples of alliteration in stanzas one and two. What effects do they have?
- How does the writer create the rhythm of the third stanza? What does that rhythm suggest?
- In the fourth stanza, the writer compares the movement of the moon with the way in which a certain animal moves. What animal is it, and what is the effect of this comparison?
- Can you pick out the main verbs in each clause? What tense are they? Can you describe the effect of this tense?
- Write down your thoughts about the haiku form in your journal. How is it different from songs and ballads? What kinds of subjects does each form cover?

WRITE YOUR OWN HAIKU

Traditionally, a haiku was written about the seasons. Choose your favourite season to write about. Picture an aspect of it in your mind; hold that picture there. Think about the atmosphere or emotions involved in your subject.

- Write a first draft of any words or phrases which come into your mind. Think back to the picture and atmosphere you want to create. Do you want to change any of your words? Keep doing this until you are satisfied with your choice of words. Try to think of some words that go together using alliteration, or try using a simile by thinking of one aspect of your subject and then thinking of something it reminds you of. Look back at the renga by Berlie Doherty – you could try words which complement each other, joining them with a hyphen as in the third verse.
- Now, try to arrange your words into three lines. Remember how many syllables are in each line of a haiku. Check your spelling and punctuation.
- When your lines are as good as you can make them, produce a final copy. Remember to give it a title, and add a photograph or drawing if possible.
- You could gather your group's haikus in a *Class Book of Haikus* which could be placed in the school library for others to read.

CINQUAIN

Another form of poetry which relies heavily on having an exact number of syllables in each line and lines in the poem is called a 'cinquain'.

'Cinquain' comes from the French word for five – cinq.

HELP

A cinquain has:
2 syllables in the first line
4 syllables in the second line
6 syllables in the third line
8 syllables in the fourth line
2 syllables in the fifth line
= 22 syllables altogether

This type of poetry was invented by the American poet Adelaide Crapsey.

Triad

These be
Three silent things:
The falling snow... the hour
Before the dawn... the mouth of one
Just dead.

November Night

Listen . . .
With faint dry sound,
Like steps of passing ghosts,
The leaves, frost-crisped, break from the trees
And fall.

Adelaide Crapsey

You can write one cinquain as a poem in its own right as Adelaide Crapsey has done, or you can write a longer piece in which each verse is a cinquain. This is what John Mole has done in his poem, 'Reflections'.

Reflections

Mirror
On the wall, is
Yours the face ill-met each
Morning? Why is it less and less
Like mine?

Keep me
(You are welcome!)
But see that I behave.
People in glass houses shouldn't
Throw stones.

Those bags
Beneath the eyes
Are packed with weariness.
Too much overnight travelling
Caused that.

Now, though,
Is not the time
For such reflections.
Mirror, your kind was never meant
To think.

Neither
Mortal spy-glass
Nor prophetic crystal –
No, you cannot tell me anything
At all.

Easy
To walk away
From mirrors, harder though
To quite forget that what's still me
Was you.

by John Mole

REFLECTIONS

What is the poet seeing in the mirror? Write down your thoughts and feelings.

- What similarities or differences can you see between cinquains, ballads, songs, haiku and renga?
- Draft and write your own cinquain, following the same process you did for your haiku.

BLANK VERSE

Blank verse is poetry that is written using a regular, repeated rhythm and line length but which doesn't necessarily rhyme. It has been one of the most widely used forms of poetry for hundreds of years and was the form Shakespeare, and many other 17th century playwrights, used for most of the speeches in their plays.

In *Hamlet*, Horatio, a soldier friend of Prince Hamlet, meets a ghostly figure on the battlements of the castle. It looks like the figure of the King, Hamlet's father, who has recently died. Horatio decides to challenge it:

Glossary

if thou art privy to
If you know the secrets of...

Horatio

But soft, behold! lo where it comes again!
Re-enter GHOST
I'll cross it, though it blast me. Stay, illusion!
If thou hast any sound, or use of voice,
Speak to me:
If there be any good thing to be done,
That may to thee do ease and grace to me,
Speak to me: [*Cock crows*
If thou art privy to thy country's fate,
Which, happily, foreknowing may avoid,
O, speak!
Or if thou hast uphoarded in thy life
Extorted treasure in the womb of earth,
For which they say, you spirits oft walk in death,
Speak of it: stay, and speak! Stop it, Marcellus.

Hamlet, Act 1, Scene 2, lines 127-139

SHAKESPEARE'S VERSE

- Working in pairs, one reading the words aloud while the other follows carefully on the page, go through the speech slowly, stopping after every two or three lines. Which words are given emphasis (spoken more strongly)? Swap roles and then discuss what you have found.
- Now read the speech in the manner of a chant while your partner beats out each syllable in a steady rhythm (perhaps using a hand on the desk, or gently tapping a drum). How many syllables are usually in a line? Which lines do not follow this pattern, and why do you think Shakespeare chose to break the pattern in this way? Discuss your ideas with the rest of your group.
- Repeat the exercise above, swapping roles, but only beat out every other syllable, beginning with the second one. For example:

```
  \      \     \        \      \
If there be an-y good thing to be done

   \       \       \        \      \
That may to thee do ease and grace to me,
```

We say that the strong syllables are 'stressed'.

HELP

Rhythm and metre

The rhythm of a poem is the regular beat formed by the poet's use of language. It is like the rhythm of music or the beat of a dance step. The rhythm can be used by a poet to create the atmosphere and pace of the poem, and to let emphasis fall on certain words.

The metre is the way in which the poet puts together stressed and unstressed syllables (strong and weak beats) to make a regular pattern. Each different metre has a different name and it is the poet's use of metre which gives the overall rhythm of the poem. The following two examples show how poets use different metres to make rhythms.

\ shows a stressed beat; x shows an unstressed beat; | | shows the pattern of the metre

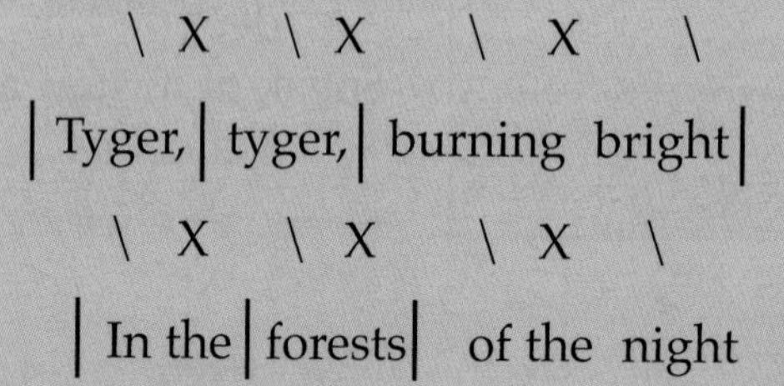

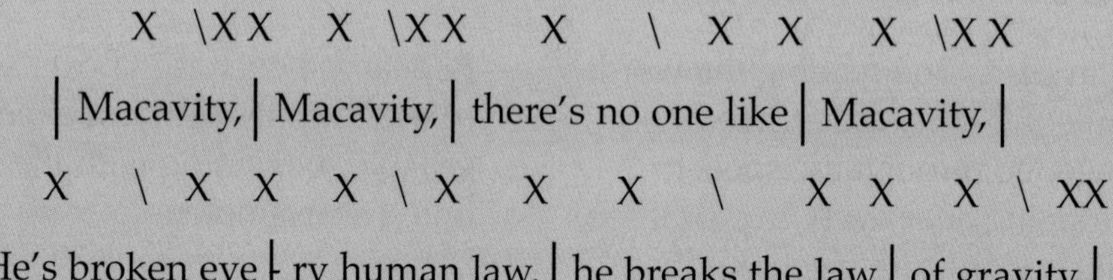

Blank verse is usually written in a metre called **iambic pentameter**. An 'iamb' is the pattern of one unstressed beat followed by one stressed beat, for example

X \ = one **iamb**
'today'

'pent' means 'five' (as in words such as 'pentagon' – a five-sided shape).
So, **iambic pentameter** has **five iambs** in a line of **ten syllables**.

RECOGNISING IAMBIC PENTAMETER

As the dawn breaks over the Danish castle, Horatio suggests that the soldiers go to tell Hamlet about the ghost.

HORATIO

But look, the morn, in russet mantel clad,
Walks o'er the dew of yon high eastward hill:
Break we our watch up; and by my advice,
Let us impart what we have seen to-night
Unto young Hamlet; for, upon my life,
This spirit, dumb to us, will speak to him.

Hamlet, Act 1, Scene 3, lines 166-171

- Read the speech aloud with a partner tapping out the stressed beats (five per line).
- Copy Horatio's speech leaving an empty line between each line of poetry. Using the empty lines, mark the stressed and unstressed syllables of iambic pentameter for each line (use a line and cross as in the examples in the help box). Make sure that you have ten syllables marked per line, five stressed and five unstressed, in the correct order for iambic pentameter. (You may choose to use different colours also.)
- Working with your partner, try writing two or more lines of blank verse about one of the following subjects: the sun going down; the moon rising; walking to school; being hungry; falling asleep. When you are both pleased with the lines (and have checked that they follow the rules of iambic pentameter), read them to the rest of your class.
- Write your thoughts about blank verse in your poetry journal. What have you learnt? How is it different from the other forms you have studied?

GRANNY GRANNY PLEASE COMB MY HAIR

by Grace Nichols

Granny Granny
please comb my hair
you always take your time
you always take such care

You put me to sit on a cushion
between your knees
you rub a little coconut oil
parting gentle as a breeze

Mummy Mummy
she's always in a hurry-hurry
rush
she pulls my hair
sometimes she tugs

But Granny
you have all the time in the world
and when you're finished
you always turn my head and say
'Now who's a nice girl.'

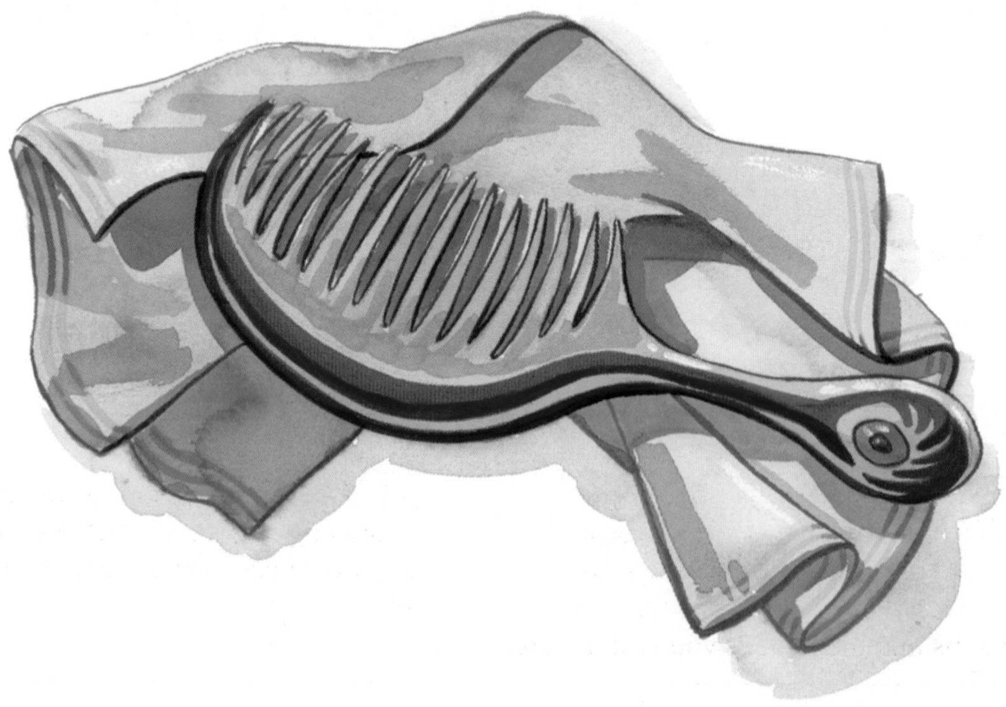

The Swans

The river runs red with the blood of many men.
The white trio with stuck out necks
Abandon the water to fly their death flight.
The trees are bare, the heavens dark,
There is no sound from the once singing lark.

Nicholas Tomkins

FREE VERSE

A poem does not have to rhyme; it does not have to be separated into verses of a particular length; it does not have to follow a set rhythm or a set line length. You can choose to write a poem as you would like it to be.

Poetry which does not follow set rules is called 'free verse'. Instead, it makes its own rules: it usually has shorter lines than prose; it may follow its own particular rhythm at certain places where the poet wants to show a link or make a point; it might contain metaphors, similes and repetition or alliteration wherever the poet wants to use them; the lines in free verse can be any length and the poet may choose to have verses of different lengths, or none at all.

HELP

Free verse – no rules for rhythm, rhyme or length.

FREE VERSE

- Read 'Granny Granny Please Comb My Hair' and 'The Swans' with a partner. Before you discuss them, note down your first reaction in your poetry journal.
- Discuss the elements of free verse, based on what you now know. Think about the differences between these poems and the ballads you read before.
- Pick out particular words or phrases you like. Discuss why you like them and why you think the poet chose those words.
- In Grace Nichols' poem, what do you think the girl's granny might be saying to her between verses 2 and 3, and verses 3 and 4?

WHAT NEXT?

In this unit you have read several different kinds of poetry and discussed some of the techniques used by poets. You have recorded your thoughts in your poetry journal and you have written some poems of your own. Think about the part you enjoyed most and about the kind of poetry you like most. You could summarise your feelings in your journal.

When you have thought back to your favourite poem or activity, read the following list and discuss with your group which further activity you would like to do. (You might decide to do one on your own.)

- Find and read Anthony Thwaite's *A Haiku Year Book* with a partner, and write a sequence of haikus, one for each month of the year. There are many other forms of poetry, such as the Tanka and Renga, which rely on having a fixed number of syllables. See if you can find out about these forms of poetry, and read some examples of them.
- Find one of the following ballads – they might be in your school library or in your local library. Read the ballad and decide how a group might perform it. Make some notes on how you think it should be performed and how any particular phrases should be read. Copy out and illustrate your favourite verse.

  'The Inchape Rock' by Robert Southey

  'The Ballad of Semmerwater' by W. Watson

  'The Highwayman' by Alfred Noyes

  'Hiawatha' by Henry Wadsworth Longfellow

  'The Revenge' by Alfred Lord Tennyson
- Browse through poetry anthologies. When you find a poem you really enjoy, copy all or a part of it, and write a brief explanation of why you like it, what techniques the poet uses and what effects are created. You could also illustrate the poem.

UNIT FOUR

Decisions, Decisions

In this unit you will assume several publishing roles. You will be, at different times, publishers, authors, designers and journalists. You will develop your skills as:

SPEAKERS AND LISTENERS

by negotiating tricky decisions about publication in a group
by collaborating as a team to produce better work
by contributing your point of view about publishing dilemmas

READERS

by comparing different versions of a piece of writing
by researching information about a real-life natural disaster
by looking for the main points in a factual piece of writing

WRITERS

by writing parts of a novel following a given outline
by learning how to target your writing for a particular audience
by writing promotional material

It takes time and money to publish a book, and the skills of many people such as writers, designers, editors, printers and booksellers. Through the following activities you are going to experience some stages in the publishing process.

PUBLISHERS AND AUTHORS

- With the help of your teacher, organise yourselves into groups of five or six. Groups will take the roles of publishers and authors in a later activity.
- Decide on a name for your publishing group. To help you, look at some of the series titles on your classroom bookshelf. Consider the way in which words are used to suggest an image: for example Good Read Books, Teenage Classics, Blast Books, Fang Books.

REVIEWING AN OUTLINE

- Read *A Time to Act*, which is an idea for a novel about battery farming. The author has submitted this outline to your publishing group for an opinion.

A TIME TO ACT

Outline for popular fiction title

The story opens with Jeremy arriving at Hightop Farm, to begin a new country life with his mother and new stepfather, Brian, who owns the farm. Jeremy is sad that his natural parents have divorced but has accepted the fact that Dan, his real father, although committed to such matters as conservation and all the world's other good causes, has been hopeless as a husband and father. Jeremy does find Brian a bit silent and thoughtful after twelve years of his father's 'sounding off', but is much more worried about going to the local comprehensive and making new friends among the 'country yokels' as he sees them.

Jeremy soon finds a friend at school – an intelligent, amusing and extremely cheeky boy called Nigel – in whose company he gets into a fair amount of trouble. Shortly after Nigel comes to tea at the farm, a new battery unit that Brian is building for the chickens (he has found free range uneconomic) is burnt down. Arson is suspected and when Jeremy discovers that Nigel is secretly passionate about animal rights, he starts to harbour doubts about his friend: could Nigel have been involved, in some way, in the fire? When interviewed by the police, however, he covers up for Nigel saying they never discussed the battery unit and never visited the site, which they did on several occasions.

Jeremy's suspicions harden when Nigel chooses to give a talk in the English lesson at school, putting forward direct action as the only way to combat animal cruelty. By this time the battery unit has been completely rebuilt. Nigel asks if he can visit again, and Jeremy is naturally very worried that Nigel will use the visit to plot the next attack. Jeremy nonetheless agrees, hoping that an explanation by Brian of the economics of the situation will start to change his views, but instead there is a furious row and the normally quiet Brian orders Nigel from the house.

Nigel goes, but shortly after he has trudged off into the night, Brian has second thoughts and jumps into the Land Rover to go and find him. Jeremy is about to go with him, then has second thoughts himself. Was the row, and his departure, deliberately staged by Nigel to get them all off the premises? As the Land Rover takes a bend, Jeremy jumps off the back down a soft bank. He races to the broiler unit and, sure enough, spies a hooded group. Voices are raised and Jeremy realises that Nigel is arguing with the fellow hooded figures, trying to stop them; yes, the row was pre-planned but he has, after all, been convinced by Brian's arguments. The leader replies that Nigel has lost his nerve. Jeremy recognises the voice. Jeremy runs forward, a fight develops, and a can of petrol is dropped and set alight. The leader catches fire, the others flee and Nigel and Jeremy help douse the hooded man. When the hood is removed Jeremy is looking at his father, Dan (animal rights is his latest cause).

By this time the hay barn is alight and sirens can be heard. Jeremy is faced by a decision: does he help his father escape or turn him over to the authorities?

THE STORYLINE

- Discuss your first reaction to the outline with your publishing group. Does it sound like a novel that would sell? Who would buy it? How do you know?
- Make a list of questions you would want to ask the author before taking matters further.
- Read the information given below about battery farming. Might it influence you in your discussion about whether to publish the novel to know that this is an issue that arouses strong emotions? Briefly discuss your own feelings about battery farms and consider how far you think the novel should 'take sides'. Why might a publisher be concerned about the point of view expressed in the novel?

BATTERY FARMING

Ninety percent of egg laying hens are housed in batteries. Batteries are large sheds where heat and light are electronically controlled to stimulate egg laying. Up to 20,000 birds are kept in cages, with four or five birds to a cage.

Feed passes in front of the cages on a conveyor belt, while droppings fall through the bottom of the cage. Eggs roll down the sloped cage onto another conveyor belt. A bird in these conditions will lay up to 260 eggs a year.

Farmers describe batteries as safe and healthy. Animal rights organisations describe conditions in batteries as cramped, cruel and unnatural.

TWO POINTS OF VIEW

The farmers' view:

- battery units give hens a balanced diet of food and water
- battery units are regularly cleaned and disinfected
- fewer hens die in batteries than in other systems

The view of animal rights organisations:

- hens are kept in cramped conditions, where they cannot spread their wings
- the hens can never carry out their normal behavioural patterns such as pecking for food or perching
- over 2 million hens die in their cages each year from injury and disease

THE WRITING

STRUCTURING THE BOOK

At the moment, the story of *A Time to Act* is simply an outline. There are no chapters and no chapter headings. Working with your group, you will now take on the role of the author.

- Look at some of the books you have read. Why are some books split into chapters? What kinds of headings are chapters given? How do chapters often start and end?
- Work out how many chapters *A Time to Act* might need. Suggest a heading for each chapter.
- In note form, jot down which parts of the story might appear in each chapter.

WRITING A SAMPLE CHAPTER

- Decide which of the chapters you are going to work on to submit to publishers as a sample (do not choose the ending). If you have long chapters, you may choose a key incident.
- Now work separately to write your own versions of this chapter.

SUBMITTING THE SAMPLE CHAPTERS

- Now give your group's sample chapters to another group.
- In your role as a publishing group, read the chapters you have received. Reach a group decision about the best version. Make notes of the reasons for your choice – you will need them.

After all the hard work of writing, writers are naturally keen to know if their work will be accepted for publication, and to get an opinion of their work. Publishers receive hundreds of books from hopeful writers. Some manuscripts are accepted but most are rejected. Nonetheless, the publishing house still sends a letter to the writer. The letter might well point out where improvements could be made and give some encouragement. Even writers whose manuscripts are accepted undergo a lengthy process to improve the book for publication.

Accepting and rejecting

- Write one acceptance letter and the rejection letters to the writers of the chapters you have received, giving constructive feedback.

Rejection letters should always:

- be polite and honest
- be tactful
- make specific points
- be constructive in criticism
- end on a positive note

HELP

Here are two examples of rejection letters.

Consider your feelings if you received each of these letters.

Watkinson Publishing,
Lion Street,
London WC2.

February 12th

Dear John,

I read your book, but I didn't like it. I like books set in towns. The countryside is boring. I thought it was silly that Jeremy's parents had got a divorce. Why wasn't he miserable anyway? I would have been. And another thing: no-one is interested in chickens!

Sorry.

Watkinson Publishing,
Lion Street,
London WC2.

February 15th

Dear John,

Thank you for submitting your manuscript, *A Time To Act*. The manuscript has been carefully read, but I am afraid we cannot accept it for publication.

I thought your opening description of the farm set the scene clearly and effectively. I also liked the idea that Jeremy had come to terms with his parents' divorce; it was unusual but sensitively handled. However, the story seemed to lack pace and drama in the middle section. Furthermore, I am not sure egg production is an issue that grabs the imagination of young people.

Thank you for submitting the manuscript to Watkinson Publishing. I wish you the best of luck for the future.

Yours sincerely,

Sonia Larding

REVISING

- When you have received back your group's chapters and letters, share your ideas for improving the accepted sample. Use the comments in the letters and the best bits out of each others' work to improve it.
- Work together to write a revised chapter.
- When you are satisfied with your new version, check it for errors.

THE ENDING

The way a book ends is very important.

Think about stories you know from books, television or films. Is there anything predictable about the way stories end? Recall endings that you found particularly satisfying, frustrating or moving and pinpoint what struck you about them.

Many readers prefer a happy ending to an unhappy ending. Sometimes writers are persuaded to change their endings, to satisfy the reading public.

One of the most famous examples is of Charles Dickens writing two endings to *Great Expectations*. In both endings Pip meets his first love, Estella, after some years.

Estella was brought up by her guardian, Miss Havisham, to break men's hearts. In the past she treated Pip very badly. Since then, Pip received a great deal of money from a secret benefactor and began to treat the people he loved as though they were beneath him.

In the first ending, Pip meets Estella by chance in the street. Estella's brutal first husband has been killed in an accident and now she is married to a poor doctor. This means, of course, that she cannot marry Pip. Estella has suffered as a result of her upbringing and, in Pip's words, 'the lady and I looked sadly on one another'.

The last sentence reads:

> 'I was very glad afterwards to have had this interview; for, in her face and in her voice, and in her touch, she gave me the assurance, that suffering had been stronger than Miss Havisham's teaching, and had given her a heart to understand what my heart used to be.'

Dickens was persuaded by a friend to change this ending. The friend thought that Dickens' first ending would upset readers. Instead, he suggested an ending where Pip and Estella would be brought together.

So Dickens, in his own words, decided to 'make the change... I have put in as pretty a little piece of writing as I could, and I have no doubt the story will be more acceptable through the alteration'.

In the second ending Pip meets Estella in the ruined grounds of Miss Havisham's old house. Estella's husband is dead and she has not remarried. So Pip and Estella could get married, if they wanted to.

> 'We are friends,' said I, rising and bending over her, as she rose from the bench.
>
> 'And will continue friends apart,' said Estella.
>
> I took her hand in mine, and we went from the ruined place; as the morning mists had risen long ago when I first left the Forge, so, the evening mists were rising now, and in all the broad expanse of tranquil light they showed to me, I saw no shadow of another parting from her.'

DECIDING AN ENDING

- Which ending to *Great Expectations* do you prefer? Why?
- Now re-read the summary of *A Time to Act*. The ending of the novel has not been given. Can you see any clues to what the ending might be? Do you feel a happy ending would be right, in view of what has happened? Or should there be an unhappy ending? Or could the ending combine happy and unhappy elements? What message is the writer trying to get across? Does that help you decide? Discuss your opinions with your group.
- Now, on your own, write the end of the novel, as you think it should be. Either write the ending in summary form or write the entire chapter. When you have finished, decide as a group which of your endings is the best and submit this to another group to get their feedback.
- Discuss any endings given to your group and give constructive feedback.
- Now read the plan of the ending actually used by the writer, at the end of this unit, and discuss it with your group. Is it the best way for the story to end, do you think?

COVER STORY

Why do books have covers? In your library you will find many different kinds of covers – not just on books, but on magazines and journals (the first and last pages of a newspaper are even termed front and back 'covers' because they serve some of the purposes of a cover). Look at as many book covers as you can and consider the different shapes, sizes, thicknesses, illustrations and details.

THE PURPOSE OF COVERS

- Having looked at the different covers of books, magazines and newspapers, make two lists: one list of as many similarities as you can find, and one list of as many differences as you can find.
- Of the book covers, which ones appeal to you the most, and why?
- What information do the book covers contain? Make a list. Next to each item of information, write down who the information is for: the reader? the writer? the publisher? the bookseller? the librarian?

- Look at the three different covers (below) for *A Time to Act*. List the differences between the covers. Decide what each cover is saying about the contents of the book. Which cover do you think would sell most copies and why?

PROMOTION

- Make a list of the last 5 books you read. How did you come by each book? Had you for example, heard of it before, or was it a gift, or a school book, or a teacher's choice? Did you see it advertised somewhere? Perhaps it was recommended in a bookshop?
- Discuss who might buy *A Time to Act* and think of as many different ways as you can in which those people might first hear about, read about, or see the book.
- If you were in charge of making sure that as many people as possible heard about the book, what might you decide to do? What considerations would you have to take into account to do these things?

PUBLISH... AND BE DAMNED?

A young boy has had an argument with his family. He stole his father's credit card and booked an airline ticket to Australia, where he was caught five days later. His story received world-wide media attention.

He wrote about his experiences and sent you the manuscript.

However, the boy's father, the police, the airline company and the press are very critical. They say that to publish is to make the boy's irresponsible action appear a clever thing to do.

A member of a top pop group has left the band. Over the past five years they have had a string of hits. The band's publicity officer knows a lot about the reasons for the split, and writes an unauthorised book about the band.

You know that you will get a lot of interest. It is likely to sell many copies to the group's fans. However, you may find yourself taken to court over some of the allegations made in the book.

You publish the works of a famous writer, Margaret West, who died long ago. While going through her papers, several early unpublished novels, short stories and poetry are found by her family. However, it is well known that Margaret did not want her early work published – she regarded it as inferior and said so in several interviews.

A writer has been extremely successful over a period of years. All his books have sold well. Now the writer has produced a new book that, in the opinion of the publishers, is well below standard: in fact, if it was a first novel submitted by an unknown writer, it would not be accepted.

The publishers have asked the writer to rewrite the book. The writer has refused, and threatened to go to a different publisher, who will accept the manuscript without changes.

Your publishing group now has a problem. If the writer goes elsewhere, you will lose a great deal of money as his books are highly profitable. On the other hand, it is completely against company policy to let a writer 'call the shots'. There are also worries about the reputation of your publishing group, if you are seen to be publishing poor material.

Your publishing house has a very clear, strong policy of promoting books by women. You have held a competition for the best new book, by a woman, about women's rights. The clear winner has been *Women First*, by an unknown writer called Janice Jones.

A day before the presentation of the award, you discover that Janice Jones is in fact John Jones – a man who had entered his book under a different name.

Do you go ahead and give John Jones his award or do you cancel everything and award the prize to a woman?

WHAT DO YOU DO?

- In your publishing group, discuss the five scenarios. You should balance the moral issues with the money-making issues. Your publishing group may go out of business if you do not make some profits.
- When you have discussed each scenario, choose the best option of all to publish. Write a report for your manager. You should give a balanced overview of why you made your choice, what the disadvantages might be, and how you would overcome them.

THE BOOK CLUB

One way to buy books is from a catalogue produced by a book club. You may have done so yourself. In the catalogue is an order form. To order a book you put a tick against the title you want, and send off the form together with the money. (Sometimes you send the money only when you receive the book.)

The catalogue will include books produced by many different publishing houses. The book club has to choose which titles it wishes to promote.

WHY USE A BOOK CLUB?

- What are the advantages of this system, compared with going to a book shop? Can you see any disadvantages? Discuss your opinions with your group.
- Now look carefully at the page from a book club catalogue. This page is taken from The Red House catalogue. The Red House is one of the biggest book clubs in Britain. Lynne Gregory is one of the people who decides which books should be promoted in the catalogue. This is what she said about Red House's publishing policy:

  'We try to encourage reading. We try to strike a balance between the popular novels, and the classic, more traditional read. There is also a balance between fiction titles and non-fiction, such as factual texts and reference books. The company also markets products such as audio tapes, videos and personal organisers. To sum up, you could say our policy at The Red House is to entertain, and educate.'
- What evidence can you find on the page to show that Lynne Gregory's policy is being put into practice? What, in your opinion, are the advantages of promoting such a wide variety of books?
- Look carefully at the page again.
  Consider:
  page design
  use of colour
  type size & type styles
  use of logos
  the way the books are described
  the kind of language used

  How do all these elements help make the books appear attractive? Are there any other ways, not mentioned in the list, that help to sell the titles?
- Consider how each of the 11 books is promoted, looking carefully at the words used.

ERIC CANTONA
CANTONA my story
WITH NEW PHOTOGRAPHS FROM THIS SEASON
39 Charismatic, controversial but a great footballer - read the story of Eric Cantona's career from his sensational arrival at Leeds United to his transfer and arrival at Manchester United up to and including this season. A bestseller new in paperback.
Paperback. 18cms x 11 cms. 235pages
£4·99
PUBLISHER'S PRICE £5.99
The Diary of ANNE FRANK
40 "I want to go on living after my death. And therefore I am grateful to God for giving me this gift ... of expressing all that is in me." The famous diary of the 13 year-old girl who, together with 7 others, went into hiding in Amsterdam when the Nazi invaders intensified their persecution of the Jews. Anne writes with inspiring courage and cheerfulness of the two dreadful years they spend in their cramped sanctuary before they were betrayed.
Paperback. 19½cms x 13cms. 256 pages.
£2·99
PUBLISHER'S PRICE £3.99
THE USBORNE BOOK OF CALLIGRAPHY PROJECTS
41 Whether you're a beginner or an experienced calligrapher, there are plenty of inspiring projects in this book that are achievable and can be done without expensive materials. Learn to make an attractive clock that really works, decorate a plate for a special occasion, print a T-shirt and much more.
Paperback. 25 cms x 20 cms. 32 pages.
£2·99
PUBLISHER'S PRICE £3.99
NOW A DEAD FUNNY TV PRODUCTION
JOHNNY AND THE DEAD
NOW A DEAD FUNNY TV PRODUCTION
42 Not many people can see the dead. Not many people would want to. But twelve-year old Johnny Maxwell can. Now the council are planning to sell their cemetery as a building-site, and they're not about to take the news lying down...
Paperback. 17cms x 10½cms. 173 pages.
£3.50
PUBLISHER'S PRICE £3.99
ELIZABETH LAIRD
Kiss the Dust
43 The terrifying journey of a Kurdish family escaping from Iraq in the 1980s - into Iran and then to London. Moving, thought-provoking and unforgettable.
Paperback. 278 pages.
£3.50
PUBLISHER'S PRICE £3.99
The Mini OXFORD SCHOOL DICTIONARY
The Mini OXFORD SCHOOL THESAURUS
44 A dictionary specially written for schools. It's mini-sized, perfect for school bags and defines over 35,000 words - with guidance on their correct usage and grammar.
Mini paperback. 11½ cms x 7½ cms. 692 pages.
£2·99
PUBLISHER'S PRICE £3.50
45 Compact and easy to use, this Thesaurus is the perfect aid to creative writing with over 150,000 similar words to expand your vocabulary.
Mini paperback. 11½ cms x 7½ cms. 806 pages.
£2·99
PUBLISHER'S PRICE £3.50
46 SPECIAL PRICE £4·99 THE PAIR
Joan Aiken
The Wolves of Willoughby Chase
49 Even the wolves that surround the great house of Willoughby Chase are not as cruel as the evil Miss Slighcarp. Bonnie and Sylvia must use all their wits if they are to escape unscathed.
Paperback. 18 cms x 11½ cms. 192 pages.
£2·50
PUBLISHER'S PRICE £2.99
HIDDEN DIMENSIONS
Use Your Deep Vision to Solve Mazes, Riddles, and Other Perplexing Puzzles
DAN DYCHMAN
GASTON LEROUX
The PHANTOM of THE OPERA
48 Look into the pages and beyond to solve the mind-boggling puzzles, riddles and mazes.
Hardback. 22½cms x 19cms. 64 pages with 64 colour illustrations.
£4·99
PUBLISHER'S PRICE £9.99
SAVE £5
THE Pooh Organiser
50 Be organised with this lovely Winnie-the-Pooh organiser. Made of sturdy card, open it up using the magnetic catch to use the Notes and Messages pad, Diary and Birthday Book - all illustrated with pictures of Pooh and his friends.
15 cms x 9½ cms.
£4·99
PUBLISHER'S PRICE £5.99
47 The classic that inspired the hugely successful musical.
Paperback. 18cms x 11½cms. 322 pages.
£2.50
PUBLISHER'S PRICE £2.99

DESIGN YOUR OWN CATALOGUE

Your publishing group will now form its own book club.

- First you must decide on a policy. To help you, look at The Red House's policy. What changes would you make for your book club? Would you choose to be a specialist book club, for example, selling only books about music or sport etc?

  Write down your policy. Two or three sentences will be enough.

- Having decided on your policy, choose or invent some titles you wish to promote in your catalogue. Now produce your own catalogue page. Remember all the elements that helped make The Red House titles look and sound attractive. Try to include at least ten titles. Sketch the covers to illustrate your catalogue.
- When you have finished your catalogue page, produce an order form for the titles you have included. Remember to include prices.
- Now pass your catalogue page and order form around the rest of the class. Each individual can order three books.
- On the basis of the orders you receive, decide which parts of your catalogue have been successful. What improvements could you make to your page, where you feel orders fell below expectations? Ask members of other groups what they liked or disliked about your catalogue page.

INFORMATION BOOKS

The next section considers how we read information books.
First, read carefully the information on the volcanic eruption at Mount St Helens, in the United States, on pages 100 and 101.

PRESENTING INFORMATION

- When you have read through the article on pages 100 and 101, imagine you are the journalist who wrote the Mount St Helens article. You have some editorial decisions to make. The layout is nearly complete, but you have a space for one extra photograph to complete two pages. You have looked in a picture library and found the following possibilities:

1 picture of Harry Truman standing in front of his lodge

2 picture of Mount St Helens before the eruption

3 picture of volcano 42 seconds into eruption

4 a map of the area around the volcano

5 aerial photo of volcano several years after eruption

Make your choice and justify it with reasons. If none of these choices were what you wanted, what other pictures do you think might appropriately fit the space?

- Write captions for the pictures in the article.

HELP

CROPPING

When a picture is used in a publication it is rarely used exactly as it was taken. Picture editors 'crop' the picture to highlight what is important and to fit the space. Pictures are either 'landscape' or 'portrait'. The space you have to fill is portrait, but a landscape picture can be cropped to fit the space. ('Landscape' means with the longer edge at the top; 'portrait' has the shorter edge at the top.)

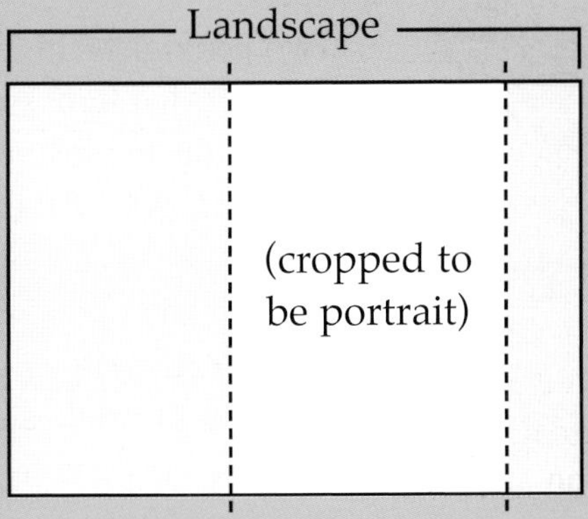

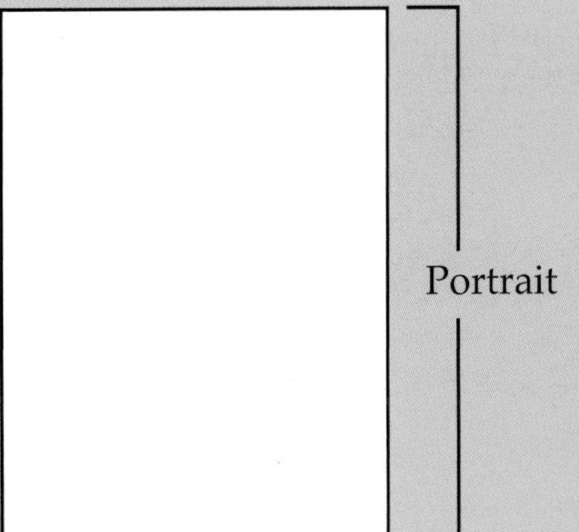

CAPTIONS

The writing underneath a photograph or picture in a book or newspaper is called a 'caption'. Captions help to interpret the main points of what is shown. Captions should not be too short: 'Volcano' under a picture of a volcano would not tell us much we did not know already!

At the same time, if a caption goes into too much detail, it distracts the reader from the picture; the place for detailed information is in the text itself.

When a mountain blew its top

Before Mount St Helens erupted on May 18th, 1980, it was a mountain nearly 3km (10,000 feet) high. Yet, so violent was the eruption, that in a matter of minutes this mountain was reduced in size by over 400m (1300 feet). Once a beautiful, snowy peak, Mount St Helens now resembles a broken off tooth.

Although there had been no eruption on Mount St Helens for 123 years, in the month before the explosion two earthquakes had taken place. During April a bulge had appeared just below the summit, that grew at the rate of a foot a day. Scientists studying the scene from the air believed the bulge to be magma rising in the heart of the volcano. An eruption was predicted, or a devastating avalanche of volcanic lava down the tree-lined slopes.

But even the scientists, the volcanologists, were taken by surprise at the scale of the eruption and following devastation. At 8.32am on May 18th a third earthquake shook the mountain, setting off the eruption. Hundreds of square kilometres of Washington State were devastated and 62 lives were lost. The death toll was relatively low because this volcano was in an area where few people lived.

Two geologists, high above the summit in a light plane, witnessed the explosion. 'The whole north side of the summit crater began to move as one gigantic mass,' they later recorded. 'The entire mass began to ripple and churn... then the whole north side of the summit began sliding...'

From the top of the mountain poured cloud and ash. An eye witness compared the cloud to a wall about three miles across. The cloud was so dense that it blocked out the sun and when it reached Washington, 402km (250

miles) away, no-one could see further than 10 feet. This ash cloud went right round the world and changed the colour of sunsets.

On the mountain itself the explosion sent an avalanche roaring down at 155mph. Huge old trees, some as tall as 50m, were flattened and snapped like matchsticks by a hurricane force wind of burning ash and hot gases. Over two million forest animals were wiped out. One of the 62 human victims was Harry Truman, aged 84, who refused to leave his home on the mountain. 'I am part of that mountain,' he said, 'the mountain is part of me.' His lodge was buried under red hot ash and his body was never found.

A cloud of gas and ash shot upward to a height of 20km (12 miles). It is estimated that 30 million tonnes of ash were thrown into the upper atmosphere. The eruption lasted nine hours and at the end the mountain top had vanished, leaving in its place a crater 1.5km (1 mile) across and 1km deep. From a beautiful snow-capped mountain it was changed in less than a day to lifeless wasteland. Scientists believe that it should remain peaceful for another 50–150 years. But with volcanoes you never can tell!

The Mount St Helens eruption claimed:
62 lives
3.7 billion board feet of lumber
5,000 black tailed deer
200 black bears
1,500 elk
all the birds and small mammals in the affected area

The energy released in the explosion was charted as being equivalent to that of 500 Hiroshima-type atomic bombs, or 10 million tons of TNT. An area of 373km (232 miles) was scorched into a moonscape.

EDITING

Two into one can go!

Your publisher has decided that the two page spread on 'Mount St Helens' must become one page. Pictures can be made smaller, but some parts of the text must be edited so that the article is shortened by at least a third.

- In pairs or groups, read through each paragraph, and decide what the main point in each one is.
- How do the rest of the sentences in each paragraph link with the main point? Could you cut them completely or cut parts of them and combine them with other sentences?

Getting the language right

A new series on volcanoes is planned with a target audience of 8–10 year olds. An appealing character called 'Volcanic Victor' will introduce readers to volcanoes in a lively stimulating way. It is planned that one page will tell the story of the Mount St Helens eruption.

- Think of the target audience. Which words would they not understand in the two-page article?
- Decide how you might reword long sentences to make them shorter and easier to read.
- Now design the layout for this page on volcanoes for younger readers, and write the first two paragraphs of the new article.

Extra Research

- Using your school's library resources, find out three facts not mentioned in the article on the Mount St Helens eruption. (Nearly every publisher has produced a book about volcanoes. Most of these published after 1980 will have pictures and references to the Mount St Helens explosion.)

HELP

Computer Search

A book is a valuable way to store information, but nowadays there are many other ways in which information is stored. Increasingly, information is stored on computer disks known as CD Roms.

When the information is put on disk, all the words used (the text) are stored in its memory. So if someone using the CD Rom wanted to find out all the information available about volcanoes, they would type in one or two key words connected with the subject. Up on the screen would come all the information in the computer's memory about volcanoes.

- Look again at the text on the Mount St Helens volcano. Which key words would you choose if conducting a computer search on volcanoes?

THE GLOSSARY

A glossary is a list of special, or technical words. A glossary of terms is often included in information books to help you understand what you are reading.

CHECKING THE MEANING

- Build up your own glossary of terms to do with writing, publishing and promotion. Listed here (right) are technical terms used in this unit. Write out their meanings and add any more terms you know already, or you discover. Put your glossary in alphabetical order.
- Find out the difference between a 'manuscript' and a 'typescript'.

Glossary of terms

text	title
caption	non-fiction
landscape	chapter
portrait	book promotion
publishing house	catalogue
edit	layout
logo	outline
crop	picture library
fiction	CD Rom

WHAT NEXT?

In this unit, you have investigated some of the elements of publishing. You have researched subjects, discussed ideas, and written your own material. You may now wish to try some of the following projects:

What do people read?

- Make a list of as many books as you can remember reading. Think back as far as you can. If you cannot remember titles, make a note of the kinds of books you enjoyed at any particular time.
- Can you remember what set you off reading certain books at particular times of your life? Discuss this with other members of your class and compare their reading experiences with yours.
- Ask an adult to tell you what they read up to your age. Can you discover anything about reading patterns now and in the past?

Ideas for a novel

- Find an idea for a novel. You might find it in a comic strip, in a poem, in an advertisement or a newspaper, or you might hear about an interesting event or see something happen in the street. Write an outline of your novel, thinking of chapter heads and an exciting ending.
- Design a cover for this novel, giving it a title, and write the summary for the back cover.
- If you have time, you might want to write a chapter of the book (or all of it!)

Your newsletter

- As a group, or as a class, compile your own school newsletter. Each member of the group should research and write a short article on a subject that interests them, or a recent event, a forthcoming event, or an ongoing issue concerning the school or the town.
- Draw pictures to go with your article and invent a caption. If you have interviewed a friend or relative, they may be able to let you have a photograph of them.
- Decide the best way to lay out all the articles in the newsletter – you may have to edit some of your text.
- Make sure the article on the front cover is the most interesting one, and include details on the front cover of what is inside.

A Time to Act – The planned ending

Dan recovers consciousness, recognises Jeremy (he had not known who had lived at the farm) and is horrified that his fanaticism could have caused his son harm. On the basis of this, Jeremy, with Nigel's help, hides his father in the farmhouse. When Brian and his mother return, he explains the situation and they, too, agree to hide and look after him. The novel ends with Jeremy saying goodbye to his father (burns healed) who is returning to London, with plans to become a teacher. From now on he will try to persuade others in a more peaceful way!

UNIT FIVE

Ernie's Incredible Illucinations

In this unit you will read and explore a complete short play. You will develop your skills as:

SPEAKERS AND LISTENERS

by acting out and improvising scenes in the play
by developing your ideas in small groups

READERS

by reading closely and predicting the text
by exploring the use of humour in the play

WRITERS

by writing a monologue
by writing dialogue that sounds like real speech

The play you are about to read is called *Ernie's Incredible Illucinations* by Alan Ayckbourn. Ernie's mum and dad take Ernie to the doctor because he has been imagining things …

BEFORE READING

- Have you ever imagined something that wasn't really true? Perhaps your eyes played tricks on you, or you imagined something so powerfully that it seemed real. Think of examples of dreams, daydreams, magic tricks, optical illusions, hypnotism and other occasions when you have imagined things that were not true.
  - In a group, share your own experiences.
  - Discuss when and why we tend to imagine things that aren't really there.

- Imagine your parents take you to the doctor because you have been having hallucinations. With a partner, improvise the scene in the doctor's surgery. Start like this:

  Doctor: Now then. What seems to be the trouble?
  You: ....

  - What do you expect a doctor to say on occasions like this?
  - How might the appointment end?

HELP

Hallucination = when somebody imagines that they see or hear something which is not really there.

Improvisation = a piece of drama performed without a script. It may change slightly each time it is rehearsed.

THE OPENING

Start to read the play.

At one side of the stage is a doctor's waiting-room. It is filled with an assortment of miserable-looking patients, coughing, wheezing, sneezing and moaning. Amongst them sit Mr and Mrs Fraser and their son, Ernie

Ernie: *(to the Audience, after a second)* If you ever want to feel ill – just go and spend a happy half-hour in a doctor's waiting-room. If you're not ill when you get there, you will be when you leave.

A man enters, having seen the doctor. He is moaning. He crosses the waiting-room and goes out. The other patients look at him and sorrowfully shake their heads.
The Receptionist enters

Receptionist Mr and Mrs Fraser …

Mum and Dad rise

Doctor will see you now.

Mum Thank you. Come on, Ernie.

Mum and Dad and Ernie follow the Receptionist across the stage to the Doctor who sits behind a table

'Morning, Doctor.

The Receptionist leaves

Doctor Ah. Ah. Mr and Mrs Fraser. Is that it?

Mum That's right. I'm Mrs Fraser – and this is my husband, Mr Fraser – and this is our son – Ernie.

Doctor Ah yes. Ernie. I've been hearing all sorts of things about you, young Ernie. Now, what have you been up to, eh?

Dad Illucinations.

Doctor Oh, yes, illuci – quite, yes.

Mum What my husband means, Doctor, is that Ernie has been creating these illusions.

Doctor Ah.

Mum Well, they're more than illusions, really.

Dad I'll say.

Doctor Beg pardon?

Dad I'll say.

Mum He's been causing that much trouble. At school, at home, everywhere he goes. I mean we can't go on like this. His dad's not as strong as he was, are you, Albert?

Dad No.

Doctor What?

Dad No.

Doctor Perhaps it would be better if you told me a little more about it. When did you first notice this …?

Mum Ah well …

Dad Ah.

Mum Now then …

Dad Now …

Mum He'd have been … well, it'd have been about … near enough … er …

Doctor Go on.

Ernie steps forward. During his speech Mum and Dad remain seated. The Doctor moves to the side of the stage, produces a notebook and makes notes on what follows

Ernie It started with these daydreams. You know, the sort everybody gets. Where you suddenly score a hat trick in the last five minutes of the Cup Final, or you bowl out the West Indies for ten runs – or saving your granny from a blazing helicopter, all that sort of rubbish. It was one wet Saturday afternoon and me and my mum and my dad were all sitting about in the happy home having one of those exciting afternoon rave-ups we usually have in our house.

Ernie sits at the table in the Doctor's chair and starts to read a book. Mum has started knitting and Dad just sits, gazing ahead of him. There is a long silence

Ernie It was all go in our house.

Pause

Mum I thought you'd be at the match today, Albert.
Dad Not today.
Mum Not often you miss a game.
Dad They're playing away.
Mum Oh.
Dad In Birmingham. I'm damned if I'm going to Birmingham. Even for United.
Ernie Meanwhile – while this exciting discussion was in progress, I was reading this book about the French wartime resistance workers and of the dangers they faced – often arrested in their homes. I started wondering what would happen if a squad of soldiers turned up at our front door, having been tipped off about the secret radio transmitter hidden in our cistern – when suddenly …

You have now met Ernie and his family.

GETTING TO KNOW THE CHARACTERS

- Sketch each person in the family and around each figure, jot down the impressions you have of their age, background, position in life, class, attitudes and character.
- The audience knows a lot about the family without being told directly. How do they know – what kind of clues are there?

USING FLASHBACKS TO TELL A STORY

- Look at Ernie's first speech 'It started with these daydreams…'. Who is 'you'?
- The play begins in the present time when Ernie's parents take him to the doctor's. What clues warn you that the story is about to slip back in time?
- Find the exact moment where we enter the past. Read the stage instructions and get into position to show where the actors are and what they are doing at the moment the play slips into the past. What does this 'freeze frame' tell us about the family?
- Do you know any other examples of stories with flashbacks? How does the transition into the past happen in them?

Read on:

ATTACK

The tramp of feet, and a squad of soldiers comes marching on and up to their front door

Officer Halte! (*He bangs on the door*)

Pause

Dad That the door?
Mum What?
Dad The door.
Mum Was it?
Officer Open zis door. Open the door! (*He knocks again*)
Mum Oh, that'll be the milkman wanting his money. He always comes round about now. Albert, have you got ten bob …?
Dad (*Fumbling in his pockets*) Ah …
Officer (*Shouting*) Open zis door immediately. Or I shall order my men to break it down! (*He bangs on the door again*)
Mum Just a minute. Coming.
Dad Should have one somewhere …
Officer We know you're in there, English spy! Come out with your hands up …!
Mum What's he shouting about? Oh, I'd better ask him for three pints next week, if Auntie May's coming …
Officer Zis is your last chance … (*He knocks again*)
Mum Oh shut up …

The Officer signals his men. Two of them step back, brace their shoulders and prepare to charge the door

I'm coming – I'm coming.
Ernie I shouldn't go out there, Mum …
Mum What?
Ernie I said don't go out there.
Mum What …?

Ernie It's not the milkman. It's a squad of enemy soldiers.
Mum Who?
Ernie They've come for me ...
Mum Who has?
Ernie The soldiers. They've found out about the radio transmitter.
Mum What radio?
Dad Hey, here, that's a point. Have you paid our telly licence yet, Ethel? It might be the detector van.
Mum Oh, sit down, Albert. Stop worrying. It's just Ernie. Shut up, Ernie.
Ernie But Mum ...
Dad I think I'll take the telly upstairs. Just in case ...

The Soldiers charge at the door. A loud crash

Ernie Don't go out, Mum.
Mum Shut up!

Dad (*picking up the television, struggling with it*) Just take it upstairs.
Ernie (*to Mum*) Don't go!
Mum I can't leave him out there. The way he's going he'll have the door off its hinges in a minute ... (*She moves to the door*)
Dad Mind your backs. Out of my way ...
Ernie Mum ...

Mum opens the door just as the two Soldiers are charging for the second time. They shoot past her, straight into the hall, collide with Dad and land in a heap with him. Dad manages to hold the television above his head and save it from breaking

Mum Hey ...
Dad Oy!

The Officer and the other Soldiers enter. Ernie crouches behind the table

Officer Ah-ha! The house is surrounded.
Mum Who are you?
Officer Put up your hands. My men will search the house.
Dad (*feebly*) Hey...
Officer (*shouting up the stairs*) We know you're hiding in here, you can't get away ...
Dad Hey – *hey* – HEY!
Officer Ah-ha. What have we here?
Dad Oh. It's the telly. The neighbour's telly. Not mine.
Officer Ah-ha.
Dad Just fixing it for him, you see ...
Officer Outside.
Dad Eh?
Officer You will come with me.
Dad What, in this? I'm not going out in this rain.
Officer Outside or I shoot.
Dad Here ...
Mum Albert ...
Ernie Hold it! Drop those guns!
Officer Ah, so ... (*He raises his gun*)
Ernie Da–da–da–da–da–da–da–da–da–da–da.

The soldiers collapse and are strewn all over the hall. Mum screams. Then there is a silence

STEREOTYPES

- The German Soldiers in this scene speak and behave in a stereotypical way – not like real soldiers but like characters from a comic strip or an old-fashioned film. Make a list of things they say and do that are stereotypical.
- The Fraser family are also stereotypes of a particular kind of English family – what is it and where else have you encountered it? Find examples of stereotypical things they say and do.
- You will be familiar with other stereotypes, particularly of different nationalities and professions. Discuss some of them and consider why we hold on to stereotypes even though we know they are inaccurate.

AUDIENCE REACTION

- What different reactions might the audience have to this scene?
- Get into fours, and break the four into pairs: one pair to find evidence that this was a figment on the imagination, and the other to find evidence that it really could have happened. First work out your case, and then argue your point of view to each other.

Now read on…

REACTIONS

Mum Oh, Ernie, What have you done?
Ernie Sorry, Mum.
Dad Oh, lad …
Mum Are they – dead?
Dad Yes.

Mum screams again

Steady, steady. This needs thinking about.

Mum What about the neighbours?
Dad Could create a bit of gossip, this could.
Mum What about the carpet? Look at it.
Dad Hasn't done that much good.
Mum What'll we do with them?
Dad Needs a bit of thinking about.

Ernie steps forward. As he speaks and during the next section, Dad and Mum carry off the bodies

Ernie Well, Mum and Dad decided that the best thing to do was to pretend it hadn't happened. That was usually the way they coped with all emergencies …

The Doctor steps forward

Mum (*struggling with a body*) We waited till it got dark, you see …

Doctor Yes? And then…?

Dad We dumped 'em.

Doctor I beg your pardon?

Dad We dumped 'em. Took 'em out and dumped em.

Doctor Dumped them? Where, for heaven's sake?

Dad Oh – bus shelters – park benches …

Mum Corporation car-park,

Dad Left one in the all-night cafeteria.

Mum And one in the Garden of Rest.

Dad Caused a bit of a rumpus.

Doctor I'm not surprised.

Mum We had the police round our way for days – trying to sort it out …

Dad They never did get to the bottom of it, though.

REACTIONS

- How is the reaction of Mum and Dad typical of them?
- Draw a picture of the doctor with a large thought bubble and fill in what he might be thinking at this point.
- Work in pairs and role play the conversation which might take place between Mum and Dad after the soldiers have been shot in their house. Write it in the style of the play, and make the characters behave as they have done so far.

HELP

SETTING OUT A PLAYSCRIPT

Plays are written to be performed on a stage in front of an audience. They have to be set out in a way which makes it easy for the actors to learn and interpret their lines.

As you read the play, be aware of how the script is set out on the page:

- name of speaker on left hand side
- new line for each speaker
- no speech marks
- stage directions in italics (and brackets – can you spot the rule for this?)
- stage directions in the present tense.

Now read on…

AUNTIE MAY

Doctor Extraordinary. And then?
Ernie (*stepping forward*) And then – Auntie May arrived to stay. I liked my Auntie May.

Auntie May enters

The Doctor steps back again

Auntie 'Ullo, Ernie lad. Have a sweetie.
Ernie Ta, Auntie. And Auntie May took me to the fair.

The stage is filled with jostling people, barkers and fairground music. The Barkers speak simultaneously

First Barker Yes, indeed, the world's tallest man! He's so tall, madam, his breakfast is still sliding down him at tea time. Come along now, sir. Come inside now …

Second Barker Ladies and gentlemen. I am prepared to guarantee that you will never again, during your lifetimes, see anything as unbelievably amazing as the Incredible Porcupine Woman. See her quills and get your thrills. Direct from the unexplored South American Jungle …

Third Barker Try your luck – come along, madam – leave your husband there, dear, he'll still be there when you come back – tell you what – if he isn't I can sell you a replacement – five shots for sixpence – knock 'em all down and pick up what you like …

Ernie Can I have a go on that , Auntie?

Auntie Not now, Ernie.

Ernie Oh go on, Auntie May.

Auntie I want a cup of tea.

Ernie Have an ice cream.

Auntie I've had three. I can't have any more. It'll bring on my condition...

Ernie What condition, Auntie?

Auntie Never you mind what. But I should never have had that candy floss as well. I'll suffer for it.

Fourth Barker Just about to start, ladies and gentlemen. A heavyweight boxing bout, featuring the one and only unofficial challenger for the heavyweight championship of the world – Kid Saracen. The Kid will be fighting this afternoon, for the very first time, a demonstration contest against the new sensation from Tyneside, Eddie 'Grinder' Edwards. In addition, ladies and gentlemen, the Kid is offering fifty pounds – yes, fifty pounds – to any challenger who manages to last three three-minute rounds…

Ernie Oh, come on, Auntie. Let's go in and watch.

Auntie What is it?

Ernie Boxing.

Auntie Boxing. I'm not watching any boxing. I don't mind wrestling but I'm not watching boxing. It's bloodthirsty.

Ernie Auntie …

Auntie Nasty stuff, boxing …

Fourth Barker Come along, lady. Bring in the young gentleman. Let him see the action …

Auntie Oh no …

Fourth Barker Come along. Two is it?

Ernie Yes please. Two.

Fourth Barker Thank you, son.

Auntie Eh?

Ernie This way, Auntie.

AUNTIE MAY

- Ernie tells us that he likes Auntie May. Why do you think he likes her? Make a list of things she says or does which please Ernie:

NOTEPAD

She gives Ernie a sweet

- The many changes of scene in this play mean that there would be little time or chance to introduce scenery and props for each shift of scene. How, then, could the impression of a fairground be achieved quickly and easily on stage? Draw a sketch that indicates to stage staff and actors how you would want to do this scene.
- What do you think might happen when Auntie May and Ernie go to the boxing match?

Now read on:

BOXING MATCH

Before Auntie May can protest, she and Ernie are inside the boxing-booth. The Crowd have formed a square around the ring in which stand Kid Saracen, Eddie Edwards and the Referee

Referee Ladies and gentlemen, introducing on my right, the ex-unofficial challenger for the World Heavyweight Championship – KID SARACEN …

Boos from the Crowd

And on my left, the challenger from Newcastle upon Tyne – EDDIE EDWARDS …

The crowd cheers

(*To the boxers*) Right, I want a good, clean fight, lads. No low blows and when I say 'break' – stop boxing right away. Good luck.

Timekeeper Seconds out.

The bell rings. The Crowd cheers as the boxers size each other up. They mostly cheer on Edwards – 'Come on, Eddie', 'Murder him, Eddie', etc. The boxers swap a few punches

Auntie Oooh. I can't look.

The man next to her starts cheering

Man Flatten him, Eddie!

Auntie peers out from behind her hands in time to see the Kid clout Eddie fairly hard

Auntie Hey, you stop that!
Man Get at him, Eddie ...!
Auntie Yes, that's right, get at him!
Man Hit him!
Auntie Knock him down.
Man Smash him! (*She starts to wave her arms about in support of Eddie, throwing punches at the air*)
Man That's it, missis. You show 'em.
Auntie I would, I would.
Man Give 'em a run for their money, would you?
Auntie I'm not that old ...
Man Eddie!
Auntie Come on, Eddie.
Ernie Eddie!

In the ring the Kid throws a terrific blow which brings Eddie to his knees

Referee One – two – three –
Man Get up, Eddie ...
Auntie Get up ... get up ...
Referee four ...

Eddie rises and blunders round the ring. The kid knocks him clean out. The Referee counts him out. The Crowd boos wildly. The Kid walks smugly round the ring, his hands above his head in triumph

Auntie You brute.
Man Boo. Dirty fight ...
Auntie Bully ...
Referee (*quietening the Crowd*) And now, ladies and gentlemen, the Kid wishes to issue a challenge to any person here who would like to try his skill at lasting three rounds – any person here. Come along now – anybody care to try ...

Muttering from the Crowd

Auntie (*to the man*) Go on then.
Man Who, me?
Auntie What are you frightened of, then?

Man I'm frightened of him ...

Referee Come along now. We're not asking you to do it for nothing. We're offering fifty pounds – fifty pounds, gentlemen ...

Auntie Go on. Fifty quid.

Man I'd need that to pay the hospital bill ...

Auntie Go on ...

Man It's alright for you, lady – just standing there telling other people to go and get their noses broken.

Auntie All right, then. I'll go in myself. Excuse me ... (*She starts to push through the Crowd towards the ring*)

Man Hey ...

Ernie Auntie, where are you going?

Auntie Out of my way ...

Man Hey, stop her – she's off her nut ...

Ernie Auntie!

Auntie (*hailing the referee*) Hey, you ...

Referee Hallo, lady, what can we do for you? Come to challenge him, have you?

Laughter from the Crowd

MONOLOGUE

- Discuss what you think might happen next.
- With a partner, discuss what Ernie might be thinking as his Auntie May makes her way to the boxing ring. Remember that he likes his Auntie May. Write Ernie's thoughts in the form of a monologue which might be inserted into the play at this point. You can describe some of the things that you think might happen next. You might start: 'I knew right away that ...'.
- Perform your monologue in front of the class, and listen to other people's.
- Together, pick out some of the best bits and discuss what made them work well.
- Then go back to your own and improve it.

HELP

Monologue = a long speech in a play which is spoken by one character alone.

Now read on:

AUNTIE IN THE RING

Auntie That's right. Help me in.

Referee Just a minute, lady, you've come the wrong way for the jumble sale, this is a boxing-ring ...

Auntie I know what it is. Wipe that silly smile off your face. Come on then, rings out of your seconds …

The Crowd cheers

Referee Just a minute. Just a minute. What do you think you're playing at …?

Auntie You said anyone could have a go, didn't you?

Referee (*getting worried*) Now, listen …

Kid Saracen Go home. There's a nice old lady …

The Crowd boos

Auntie You cheeky ha'porth

Second man Hit him, grandma.

The Crowd shouts agreement

Referee Tell you what, folks. Let's give the old lady fifty pence for being a good sport …

Auntie I don't want your fifty pence … Come on.

Woman Get the gloves on, granny.

Auntie I don't need gloves. My hands have seen hard work. I was scrubbing floors before he was thought of.

Woman That's right, love.

Ernie (*stepping forward*) And then suddenly I got this idea. Maybe Auntie May could be the new heavyweight champion of the world …

The bell rings. Auntie May comes bouncing out of her corner flinging punches at the Kid, who looks startled. The Crowd cheers

Auntie Let's have you.

Kid Saracen Hey, come off it!

The Referee tries vainly to pull Auntie May back but she dances out of reach

Kid Saracen Somebody chuck her out.

The Kid turns to appeal to the Crowd. Auntie May punches him in the back

Auntie Gotcher!

Kid Saracen Ow!

Auntie May bombards the Kid with punches

Ernie (*commentator style*) And Auntie May moves in again and catches the Kid with a left and a right to the body and there's a right-cross to the head – and that really hurt him – and it looks from here as if the champ is in real trouble ... as this amazing sixty-eight-year-old challenger follows up with a series of sharp left-jabs – one, two, three, four jabs ...

The Kid is reeling back

And then, bang, a right-hook and he's down ...!

The Kid goes down on his knees. The Crowd cheers

Auntie (*to the Referee*) Go on. Start counting.
Crowd One – two – three – four – five – six ...

The Kid gets up again

Ernie And the Kid's on his feet but he's no idea where he is – and there's that tremendous right uppercut – and he's down again ...!

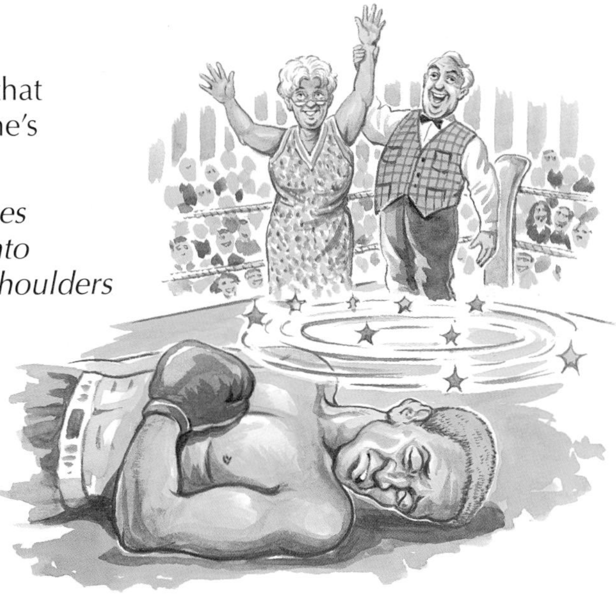

The Crowd counts him out. Auntie May dances round the ring with glee. The Crowd bursts into the ring and Auntie May is lifted on to their shoulders

The Crowd go out with Auntie May, singing 'For She's a Jolly Good Fellow'. The Referee and the Kid are left

Referee Come on. Get up – Champ.

Kid Saracen Ooooh. (*He staggers to his feet*)

The Kid goes out, supported by the Referee. Ernie, Dad, Mum and the Doctor are left

Doctor (*Still writing, excitedly*) Absolutely incredible!

Mum Terrible it was. It took it out of her, you know. She was laid up all Sunday.

Dad And we had all those fellows round from the Amateur Boxing Association trying to sign her up to fight for the Combined Services.

Mum So I told his dad on the Monday, seeing as it was half-term, 'Take him somewhere he won't get into trouble,' I said. 'Take him somewhere quiet'.

Dad So I took him down to the library.

The Doctor retires to the side of the stage again. Dad, Mum and Ernie exit

THINGS THAT MAKE US LAUGH

- Brainstorm some of the things which make you laugh.

- Organise your ideas into categories of different types of humour
  e.g
  Sarcasm
  Slapstick
- Identify the things that will make sure the audience laugh in the scene with Auntie May.
  e.g.
  Silly rhymes ('See her quills and get your thrills.')

THE COMMENTARY

- Look again at Ernie's speech which is described as 'commentator style'. Name some famous commentators, and explain what they do.
- List the features of 'commentator style', by studying:
  - the length of the sentences
  - the punctuation
  - the expressions used
  - the use of the word 'and'
  - the pace of the piece
- Write a short commentary on one of the following:
  - a football match
  - an English lesson
  - a family meal

WHAT NEXT?

- Brainstorm what might happen when Dad takes Ernie to the library.
- Then discuss how you made your prediction. How do you know what to expect? Discuss:
  - what you already know about plays and the way they unfold
  - what has happened already
  - what can be ruled out

Now read on…

AT THE LIBRARY

The scene becomes the Public Library. It is very quiet. Various people tip-toe about. At one end sits an intellectual-looking Lady with glasses, reading; at the other, an old Tramp eating his sandwiches from a piece of newspaper. One or two others. A uniformed Attendant walks up and down importantly. The Lady with glasses looks up at the lights. She frowns

Lady Excuse me …

Attendant Sssshhh!

Lady Sorry. (*Mouthing silently*) The light's gone.

Attendant (*mouthing*) What?

Lady (*whispering*) I said the light's gone over here.

Attendant (*whispering*) What?

Lady New bulb.

The Attendant shakes his head, still not understanding

Loudly UP THERE! YOU NEED A NEW BULB - IT'S GONE. I CAN'T SEE!

People Sssshhh!

Attendant (*whispering*) Right.

Lady (*whispering*) Thank you.

The Attendant tip-toes out as Dad and Ernie tip-toe in

Dad (*to Ernie*) Sssshhhh!

Ernie nods. They tip-toe and sit

Ernie (*to the Audience*) I didn't really think much of this idea of my mum's …

People Ssssshhh!

Ernie (*whispering*) I didn't really think much of this idea of my mum's. It was a bit like sitting in a graveyard only not as exciting. The trouble is, in library reading-rooms some bloke's pinched all the best magazines already and you're left with dynamic things like *The Pig Breeder's Monthly Gazette* and suchlike. I'd got stuck with *The Bell Ringer's Quarterly.* Which wasn't one of my hobbies. Nobody else seemed to be enjoying themselves either.
Except the bloke eating his sandwiches in the corner. I reckoned he wasn't a

tramp at all, but a secret agent heavily disguised, waiting to pass on some secret documents to his contact who he has to meet in the library and who was at this very moment lying dead in the Reference Section, a knife in his ribs. Realising this, the tramp decides to pick on the most trustworthy-looking party in the room – my dad!

The Tramp gets up stealthily and moves over to Dad. As he passes him he knocks his magazine out of his hand

Dad Hey!

Tramp Beg pardon, mister. (*He bends to pick up the magazine and hands it back to Dad. As he does so he thrusts his newspaper parcel into Dad's hands*) Sssshhhh. Take this. Quickly! They're watching me. Guard it with your life.

Dad Eh?

The Tramp hurries away. A sinister man in a mackintosh gets up and follows him out

Who the heck was that?

Ernie Dunno, dad.

Dad (*examining the parcel*) What's all this, then?

Ernie Dunno.

Dad I don't want his sandwiches. Spoil my dinner (*As he unwraps the parcel*) Hey!

Ernie What is it?

Dad Looks like a lot of old blue-prints and things. Funny. This anything to do with you?

Ernie (*innocently*) No, Dad.

The Attendant enters with a step-ladder. He places it under the light. A Girl Librarian who has entered with him steadies the step-ladder. The Attendant produces a bulb from his pocket and starts to climb the step-ladder

(*Watching the Attendant*) And now, as Captain Williams nears the summit of this, the third highest mountain in the world, never before climbed by man …

Wind noises start

He pauses for a moment through sheer exhaustion …

The Attendant, feeling the effects of the wind, clings to the step-ladder for dear life. It sways slightly

Attendant (*shouting down to the Librarian*) More slack. I need more slack on the rope …!

Librarian (*shouting up to him*) More slack. Are you all right?

Attendant I – think – I can – make it.

Librarian Be careful. The rocks look treacherous just above you.

Attendant It's all right. It's – quite safe – If I – just aaaaahhh!

(*He slips and holds on with one hand*)

Lady Captain. What's happened?

Attendant Damn it. I think I've broken my leg …

Lady Oh, no.

Librarian How are we going to get him down?

HALLUCINATIONS

- At the beginning of this unit you shared experiences of 'hallucinating' with others in your group. Now think carefully about Ernie's hallucinations:
  - the German soldiers
  - the boxing match
  - the secret agent
  - the mountain rescue
- Work out why Ernie has these hallucinations. Consider:
  - what they have in common
  - the kind of boy he is
  - the kind of life he leads
  - what is going on inside his mind
- Share your ideas.
- Imagine Ernie is a girl – short for Ernestina! What kind of fantasies would she have?
- Discuss why it is that boys and girls have different hopes and dreams.

Read on …

RESCUE

Dad rises

Ernie And here comes Major Fraser, ace daredevil mountaineer, to the rescue.

Dad Give me a number three clambering-iron and a hydraulic drill-lever, will you? I'm going up.

Librarian Oh no, Major.

Dad It's the only way.

Lady Don't be a fool, Major.

Dad Someone's got to go. Give me plenty of line … (*He starts to climb*)

Librarian Good luck.

Lady Good luck.

A sequence in which Dad clambers up the ladder, buffeted by the wind

Dad Can you hold on?

Attendant Not – much – longer.

Dad Try, man, try. Not much longer …

Lady Keep going, man.

Dad reaches the Attendant. People cheer. The two men slowly descend the ladder

Ernie And here comes the gallant Major Fraser, bringing the injured Captain Williams to safety …

Dad and the Attendant reach the floor. More cheers and applause from the onlookers. The Attendant is still supported by Dad with one arm round his neck. There is a general shaking of hands. The wind noise stops

Attendant (*Coming back to reality, suddenly*) Hey, hey! What's going on here? (*to Dad*) What do you think you're doing?

Dad Oh.

Attendant Let go of me.

Dad Sorry, I …

Attendant Never known anything like it. This is a public building, you know …

Dad Ernie ...
Ernie Yes, Dad?
Dad Did you start this?
Ernie (*innocently*) Me, Dad?
Dad Now listen, lad...
A Second Librarian enters, screaming
Second Librarian Oh, Mr Oats, Mr Oats ...
Attendant What's the matter, girl? What's the matter?
Second Librarian There's a man in the Reference Section.
Attendant Well?
Second Librarian He's dead.
Lady Dead?
Second Librarian Yes. I think he's been killed. There's a knife sticking in his ribs ...
The First Librarian screams. The Attendant hurries out, followed by the others. Ernie and Dad are left
Dad Ernie!
Ernie Sorry, Dad.
The Doctor moves in. Mum joins them
Doctor Incredible.
Dad Embarrassing.
Doctor Yes, yes.

DIALOGUE

Here is a transcript of real speech recorded in writing:

First girl: Well ... she ... um ... she didn't really know ... no ... I don't think she ...
Second girl: No ... she couldn't have ... mmm ...
First girl: But I don't see why she ... she couldn't have ... (*pause*) ... told us
Second girl: No
First girl: No

- This is what real speech actually sounds like. Think of five ways in which it is different from speeches in a play.
- Listen to some real conversations. You will notice that when people speak to each other in everyday conversations, they do some of the following:
  - hesitate
  - repeat sounds
  - use fillers like 'um' when they are thinking about what to say next
  - interrupt
  - make sounds which show they agree with the other person ('mmm')
  - lose the thread
  - use colloquial expressions
  - shorten words e.g. 'can't' for 'cannot'

Playwrights invent, shape and polish speech, but to make it sound convincing they often borrow some of the characteristics of everyday speech.

DIALOGUE TECHNIQUES

Look at two full pages of the play so far and find examples of Alan Ayckbourn using features of everyday speech to make the dialogue seem real. Set your findings out in a chart like this:

Technique used	Example
Colloquial language	Give 'em a run for their money, would you?

PREPARING FOR THE ENDING

- Work in a small group to discuss how the play might end.
- How will the doctor diagnose Ernie's condition? Will he:
  - believe him?
  - cure him?
  - dismiss it all as nonsense?
  - have an hallucination himself?
- Agree on the best idea in your group and improvise the scene.
- Rehearse your improvisation and turn it into a short playscript. If possible, learn your lines and present the scene to the rest of the class.
- As you read on, compare your own playscript with the original.

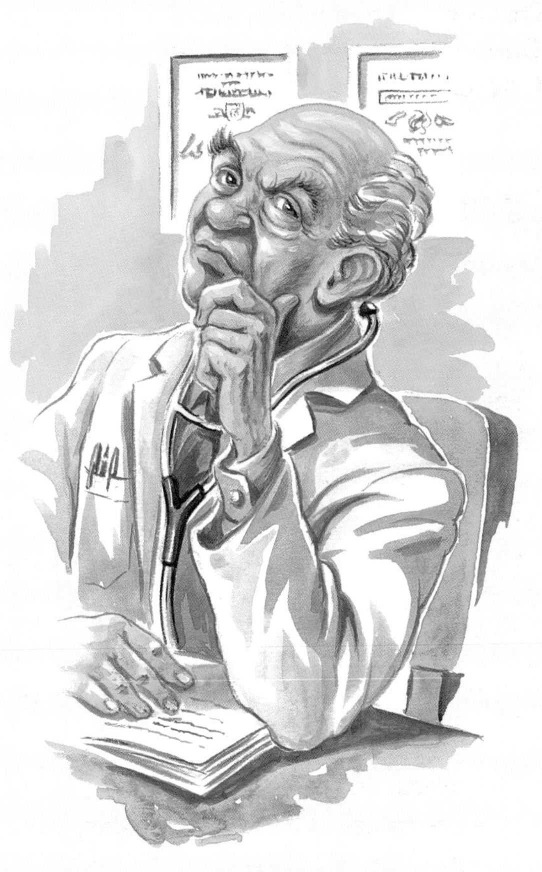

THE ENDING

The scene is now back to where it was at the beginning, with the four in the Doctor's room on one side and the waiting-room full of patients on the other

Mum Can you do anything, Doctor?
Doctor Mmmm. Not much, I'm afraid.
Mum No?
Doctor You see, it's not really up to me at all. It's up to you. An interesting case. Very. In my twenty years as a general practitioner I've never heard of anything quite like it. You see, this is a classic example of group hallucinations ...
Dad Illucinations, yes.
Doctor Starting with your son and finishing with you all being affected ...
Mum All?
Doctor All of you. You must understand that all this has happened only in your minds.
Dad Just a minute. Are you suggesting we're all off our onions?
Doctor Off your ...?
Dad You know. Round the thing. Up the whatsit.
Doctor No ...
Dad My missis as well?
Doctor No. No.
Dad Then watch it.
Doctor I was just explaining ...
Dad You don't need. It's Ernie here, that's all. He imagines things and they happen.
Doctor Oh, come now. I can't really accept that.
Dad Why not?
Doctor It's – impossible. He may *imagine* things ...
Dad He does.
Doctor But they don't *really* happen. They *appear* to, that's all.
Dad Is that so?
Doctor Of course.

A slight pause

Dad Ernie.
Ernie Yes, Dad.
Dad Imagine something. We'll see who's nutty.
Ernie What, Dad?
Dad Anything, son, anything. Just to show the doctor.
Mum Nothing nasty, Ernie. Something peaceful...
Dad How about a brass band? I like brass bands.
Mum Oh dear. Couldn't it be something quieter? Like – a mountain stream or something ...
Dad Don't be daft, Ethel. The Doctor doesn't want a waterfall pouring through his surgery. Go on, lad. A brass band.
Ernie Right, Dad. (*He concentrates*)

A pause

Doctor Well?
Dad Give him a chance.

A pause

Mum Come on Ernie. (*Pause*) He's usually very good at it, Doctor.
Dad Come on, lad.
Ernie It's difficult, Dad, I can't picture them.
Doctor Yes, well I'm afraid I can't afford any more time just now, Mr and Mrs Fraser. I do have a surgery full of people waiting to see me – (*he calls*) – Miss Bates! – so you will understand I really must get on.

The Receptionist enters

Receptionist Yes, Doctor?
Doctor The next patient, please, Miss Bates.
Receptionist (*going*) Yes, Doctor.

Receptionist exits

Doctor (*getting up and pacing up and down as he speaks*) What I suggest we do is, I'll arrange an appointment with a specialist and – he'll be able to give you a better diagnosis – (*his steps become more and more march like*) – than I will. I'm quite sure – that – a – few – sessions – with a trained – psychiatrist – will – be – quite – sufficient – to put – everything – right – right – left – right – left – left – left – right – left …

The Doctor marches to the door of his room, does a smart about-turn and marches round his desk

The patients from the waiting-room enter and follow him, some limping, some marching and all playing, or as if playing, brass instruments

L-e-e-e-ft … Wheel …

After a triumphal circuit of the room everyone marches out following the Doctor, who has assumed the role of drum major

Ernie (*just before he leaves*) It looks as though the Doctor suffers from illucinations as well. I hope you don't get 'em. Ta-ta.

Ernie marches out jauntily, following the band, as – the CURTAIN falls

ON REFLECTION

- Discuss your reactions to the ending. Was it more or less satisfying than your own?
- There is another sense in which the play is about hallucination. The play itself is a fiction or fantasy by the writer which is brought to life for the audience by the actors. It is itself a sort of deliberate hallucination. Where else in life do we come across imagined experiences of this sort?
- Human beings, unlike animals, have the power to imagine how things could be different, and to make-believe they are. Why is it useful and satisfying to be able to do this? Why has it made us such a successful species?

WHAT NEXT?

Bringing the play to life

- Design a stage set for the play. You will need to provide an area of the stage for 'real time' as well as an area for the 'hallucinations'. You will need to consider how the actors will enter and leave the stage as well as the props they will need.
- Imagine you are the director for a new production of the play. Decide which actors and actresses you would cast in the leading roles and why.
- Direct a scene. Work in groups of four or five and choose a section of the play to work on e.g. the soldiers or Auntie May and Kid Saracen. Allocate parts and decide what advice you would give to the actors playing the parts. You should consider:
  - the way they speak their lines
  - the way they move about on stage
  - the way they respond to other characters on the stage
  - what they should be doing when they are not speaking a line.
- Later, groups can watch each others' productions. As you watch other groups perform their work, try to evaluate their success. The following prompts might help you:
  - how effectively did they bring out the humour in the scene?
  - did they seem to be 'in role' all of the time?
  - how did they keep the audience's attention?

Extension writing

Either

- write another scene for the play in which Ernie has another hallucination

Or

- imagine that the play is called 'Ernestina's Incredible Illucinations', and write a scene for the play in which the main character is a girl and the hallucinations are stereotypically female.

UNIT SIX

Dear Diary

In this unit, you will look at different styles and purposes of diary writing. You will also practise writing diary entries for personal use and for others to read. You will develop your skills as:

SPEAKERS AND LISTENERS

by sharing personal experiences
by brainstorming ideas together
by becoming a 'critical friend' in order to help somebody else improve the quality of their writing

READERS

by studying a range of different approaches to the writing of diaries and journals
by recognising different styles and learning how to use them
by reading aloud in a variety of ways

WRITERS

by recording initial thoughts and ideas
by experimenting with a range of 'diary' styles
by adapting your first drafts for other people to enjoy

You are about to begin a journey. This journey will be about YOU: your world, your memories. It will allow you to share your thoughts and feelings and to record your secrets. It will even allow you to become somebody else.

A diary is a place to write about experience, chiefly for your own benefit. In writing, you attempt to preserve past experience and to understand it better. Choosing words and putting them in order brings discipline to jumbled experience.

It is not surprising that many great writers began by making regular entries in a diary. There they learned the craft of writing true-to-life stories by observing what is interesting in everyday life.

The subject need not be grand. Everyday life is made fascinating in its own right by the diary writer, but it can be surprisingly difficult to capture the exact flavour of events. Many diary writers comment that writing gives them unexpected insights into ordinary life, so it is worth the effort.

Letters, reports and some stories are written in the first person as 'I'. So are diaries but, unlike these other forms, they are intended for an unusual audience: oneself. It follows that the main function of keeping a diary is to cast light on your own life

THE COVER STORY

This diary will be yours and yours alone. Make a cover to reflect your life, personality and interests. A simple diary can be made by folding plain A4 paper, and using a hole punch to fit treasury tags. The cover should be slightly bigger, and made of card.

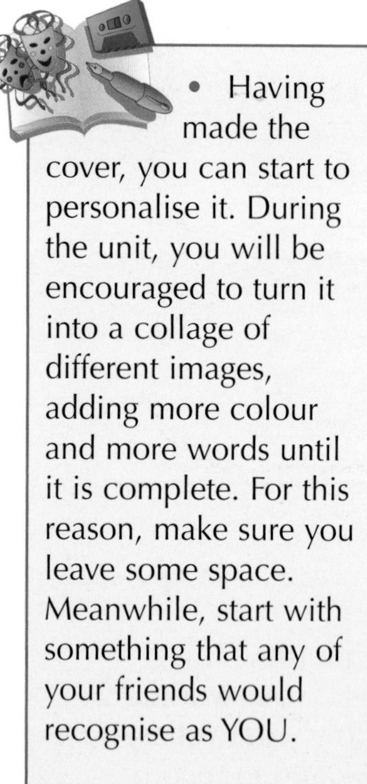

- Having made the cover, you can start to personalise it. During the unit, you will be encouraged to turn it into a collage of different images, adding more colour and more words until it is complete. For this reason, make sure you leave some space. Meanwhile, start with something that any of your friends would recognise as YOU.

YESTERDAY

- Working with a partner, take it in turns to ask each other about what happened yesterday. What do you particularly remember? What did you do and when? Encourage each other to tell all, and then swap roles to see if you can remember what happened to each other.

Dear Diary

- Round a clock face (of you, perhaps) draw time bubbles into which you can fit actions, events and happenings that occurred yesterday.

Dear Diary

- Use the ideas from your 12 hour clock face to help you write your first diary entry. What would you write about yesterday? How would you begin?

HELP

ADDING COLOUR TO YOUR WRITING

You can make your writing interesting visually and in the details you give which help to create a mental picture of you and your lifestyle.

Got up	*Finally managed to drag myself out of bed...*
Got dressed	*Chose the shirt I bought on Saturday... Told to take it off – not suitable for school, not school uniform. Ugh!...*
Felt fed up	*If only I was older and didn't have to do everything I was told, go to school, be on time...*
Had breakfast Went to school Maths lesson Breaktime More lessons Lunch	?

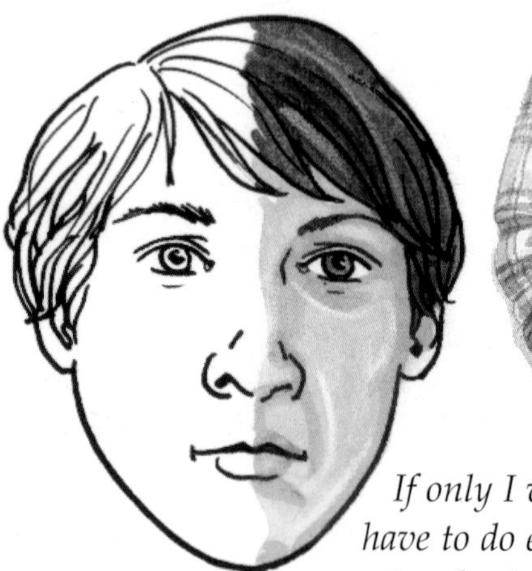

What makes the writing on the right more interesting? What could be written further down the page?

What details could be added to the accounts on the right to give an even clearer picture?

Even when they are writing about ordinary days, diary writers often add the kind of detail that makes things come alive for the reader.

Monday, 2 September 1991
Behind me – a long, hot summer and the happy days of summer holidays; ahead of me – a new school year. I'm starting fifth grade. I'm looking forward to seeing my friends at school, to being together again. Some of them I haven't seen since the day the school bell rang, marking the end of term. I'm glad we'll be together again, and share all the worries and joys of going to school.

Mirna, Bojana, Marijana, Ivana, Maša, Azra, Minela, Nadža – we're all together again.

Tuesday, 10 September 1991
This week was spent getting my books and school supplies, describing how we spent our holidays on the seaside, in the mountains, in the countryside and abroad. We all went somewhere and we all have so much to tell one another.

Thursday, 19 September 1991
Classes have also started at music school now. I go twice a week for piano and solfeggio. I'm continuing my tennis lessons. Oh yes, I've been moved up to the 'older' group in tennis. Wednesdays I go to Auntie Mika's for English lessons. Tuesdays I have choir practice. Those are my responsibilities. I have six lessons every day, except Fridays. I'll survive...

Monday, 23 September 1991
I don't know if I mentioned my workshop class (it's a new subject) which starts in fifth grade. Our teacher is Jasmina Turajilić and I LIKE HER. We learn about wood, what it is, how it's used, and it's pretty interesting. Soon we'll be moving on to practical work, which means making various things out of wood and other materials. It'll be interesting.

Friday, 27 September 1991
I'm home from school and I'm really tired. It's been a hard week. Tomorrow is Saturday and I can sleep as long as I like. LONG LIVE SATURDAYS!

From *Zlata's Diary* by Z. Filipović

ZLATA'S DIARY

- Working with a partner, decide how old you think the writer is and where she comes from.
- What do you know about the writer's character from reading these extracts? Make a list and note down which phrases give you clues.

Dear Diary

- What could you now add to yesterday's entry to make it more colourful and interesting? Write your additions on the page opposite, using arrows to show how it fits in.

The tone of your writing need not always be serious but should reflect your character. Even the most light-hearted diaries can be very revealing...

Thursday January 1st

BANK HOLIDAY IN ENGLAND, IRELAND, SCOTLAND AND WALES

These are my New Year's resolutions:

1. I will help the blind across the road.
2. I will hang my trousers up.
3. I will put the sleeves back on my records.
4. I will not start smoking.
5. I will stop squeezing my spots.
6. I will be kind to the dog.
7. I will help the poor and ignorant.
8. After hearing the disgusting noises from downstairs last night, I have also vowed never to drink alcohol.

My father got the dog drunk on cherry brandy at the party last night. If the RSPCA hear about it he could get done. Eight days have gone by since Christmas Day but my mother still hasn't worn the green lurex apron I bought her for Christmas! She will get bathcubes next year.

Just my luck, I've got a spot on my chin for the first day of the New Year!

Friday January 2nd

BANK HOLIDAY IN SCOTLAND. FULL MOON

I felt rotten today. It's my mother's fault for singing 'My Way' at two o'clock in the morning at the top of the stairs. Just my luck to have a mother like her. There is a chance my parents could be alcoholics. Next year I could be in a children's home.

The dog got its own back on my father. It jumped up and knocked down his model ship, then ran into the garden with the rigging tangled in its feet. My father kept saying, 'Three months' work down the drain', over and over again.

The spot on my chin is getting bigger. It's my mother's fault for not knowing about vitamins.

THE SECRET DIARY OF ADRIAN MOLE

- In groups of four, discuss the first two extracts from *The Secret Diary of Adrian Mole* (above). Two members of the group should look at the first extract, and the other two take the second. Make notes of the things you learn about Adrian Mole – his sense of humour, his feelings about his family, his likes or dislikes, and his general appearance. Swap lists with the other two members of your group and see if you can add anything to what they have spotted from their extract.
- Brainstorm ways in which the writer makes Adrian Mole's diary amusing and colourful in all three extracts. Look at *how* events are written as well as what is written. What do you find funny about they way they are written?

Class Four-D's Trip to the British Museum

7am Boarded coach.
7.05 Ate packed lunch, drank low-calorie drink.
7.10 Coach stopped for Barry Kent to be sick.
7.20 Coach stopped for Claire Neilson to go to the Ladies.
7.30 Coach left school drive.
7.35 Coach returned to school for Ms Fossington-Gore's handbag.
7.40 Coach driver observed to be behaving oddly.
7.45 Coach stopped again for Barry Kent to be sick again.
7.55 Approached motorway.
8.00 Coach driver stopped coach and asked everyone to stop giving 'V' signs to lorry drivers.
8.10 Coach driver loses temper, refuses to drive on motorway until 'bloody teachers control kids'.
8.20 Ms Fossington-Gore gets everyone sitting down.
8.25 Drive on to motorway.
8.30 Everyone singing 'Ten Green Bottles'.
8.35 Everyone singing 'Ten Green Snotrags'.
8.45 Coach driver stops singing by shouting very loudly.
9.15 Coach driver pulls in at service station and is observed to drink heavily from hip-flask.
9.40 Barry Kent sick in coach.
9.50 Two girls sitting near Barry Kent are sick.
9.51 Coach driver refuses to stop on motorway.
9.55 Ms Fossington-Gore covers sick in sand.
9.56 Ms Fossington-Gore sick as a dog.
10.30 Coach crawls along on hard shoulder, all other lanes closed for repairs.
11.30 Fight breaks out on back seat as coach approaches end of motorway.
11.45 Fight ends. Ms Fossington-Gore finds first-aid kit and sees to wounds. Barry Kent is punished by sitting next to driver.
11.50 Coach breaks down at Swiss Cottage.
11.55 Coach driver breaks down in front of AA man.
12.30 Class Four-D catch London bus to St Pancras.
9.30 Barry Kent hands round bars of chocolate stolen from self-service shop at service station.
Ms Fossington-Gore chooses Bounty bar.

From *The Secret Diary of Adrian Mole* by Sue Townsend

HELP

Colourful punctuation

Most diaries are in a fairly informal kind of writing, so punctuation can be used in interesting and unusual ways. The following exercise shows the differences made by punctuation.

> *Saturday April 17th*
> Still in bed with toothache my parents are showing me no sympathy they keep saying you should have gone to the dentists I have phoned Pandora she is coming round tomorrow she asked me if I needed anything I said a Mars bar would be nice she said quite irritably I thought heavens above Adrian aren't your teeth rotten enough the dog has been howling outside Mitzi's gate all day it is also off its Pedigree Chum and Winalot

- Try reading this extract to each other.

REMEMBER
- You cannot take a breath!
- You cannot change your tone!
- You cannot pause, until the end!

> *Saturday April 17th*
> Still in bed with toothache. My parents are showing me no sympathy they keep saying you should have gone to the dentists. I have phoned Pandora she is coming round tomorrow. She asked me if I needed anything I said a Mars bar would be nice. She said quite irritably I thought heavens above Adrian aren't your teeth rotten enough. The dog has been howling outside Mitzi's gate all day. It is also off its Pedigree Chum and Winalot.

- Now experiment with reading this one. (Try reading it as robot might speak.)

REMEMBER
- Pause ONLY at full stops!
- No change of voice or tone!
- No change of volume or emphasis!

> *Saturday April 17th*
> Still in bed with toothache.
> My parents are showing me no sympathy, they keep saying, 'You should have gone to the dentist's'.
> I have phoned Pandora: she is coming round tomorrow. She asked me if I needed anything; I said a Mars bar would be nice. She said (quite irritably I thought), 'Heavens above, Adrian, aren't your teeth rotten enough?'
> The dog has been howling outside Mitzi's gate all day. It is also off its Pedigree Chum and Winalot.

- Is the second version better than the first?
- Read this extract aloud in as many different ways as you can.

REMEMBER
- Pause where the punctuation indicates!
- Change the tone, emphasis and volume to make it as interesting as possible!

- In what ways is the third version better?
- What does the punctuation *do*?
- Look back at the extracts from *Zlata's Diary* and *The Secret Diary of Adrian Mole*. What other kinds of punctuation are used?

Dear Diary

- Invent a day! Call it 'If only....' and make it the most exciting day you can imagine. Try to use different styles of writing – you could include lists or dialogue for example, or add a cartoon strip.

TURNING POINTS

Diaries can also be used to write about turning points in your life. They provide an opportunity to record and come to turns with the 'ups and downs' of life.

For some people, the turning points are caused by major events outside their control, things you might only hear about in the news. Zlata lives in Sarajevo, in the former Yugoslavia. She recorded in her diary what the war meant for her and her family:

Wednesday, 27 May 1992

Dear Mimmy,
SLAUGHTER! MASSACRE! HORROR! CRIME! BLOOD! SCREAMS! TEARS! DESPAIR!

That's what Vaso Miskin Street looks like today. Two shells exploded in the street and one in the market. Mummy was near by at the time. She ran to Grandma's and Grandad's. Daddy and I were beside ourselves because she hadn't come home. I saw some of it on TV but I still can't believe what I actually saw. It's unbelievable. I've got a lump in my throat and a knot in my tummy. HORRIBLE. They're taking the wounded to the hospital. It's a madhouse. We kept going to the window hoping to see Mummy, but she wasn't back. They released a list of the dead and wounded. Daddy and I were tearing our hair out. We didn't know what had happened to her. Was she alive? At 16.00, Daddy decided to go and check the hospital. He got dressed, and I got ready to go to the Bobars', so as not to stay at home alone. I looked out the window one more time and . . . I SAW MUMMY RUNNING ACROSS THE BRIDGE. As she came into the house she started shaking and crying. Through her tears she told us how she had seen dismembered bodies. All the neighbours came because they had been afraid for her. Thank God, Mummy is with us. Thank God.

A HORRIBLE DAY. UNFORGETTABLE. HORRIBLE! HORRIBLE!
Your Zlata

Thursday, 28 May 1992

Dear Mimmy,
It started at around 22.00. First we went to Neda's. I put Saša to sleep and left the bedroom. I looked towards the loo, and then ... BOOM. The window in the loo shattered into pieces and I was alone in the hall and saw it all. I began to cry hysterically. Then we went down into the cellar. When things calmed down we went up to Neda's and spent the night there. Today in Vaso Miskin Street people signed the book of mourning and laid flowers. They renamed the street and now its called the Street of Anti-Fascist Resistance.
Zlata

Friday, 29 May 1992

Dear Mimmy,
I'm at Neda's. The result of last night's fascism is broken glass in Daddy's office and Bobar's shattered windows. A shell fell on the house across the way, and I can't even tell you how many fell near by. The whole town was in flames.
Your Zlata

Saturday, 30 May 1992

Dear Mimmy,
The City Maternity Hospital has burned down. I was born there. Hundreds of thousands of new babies, new residents of Sarajevo, won't have the luck to be born in this maternity hospital now. It was new. The fire devoured everything. The mothers and babies were saved. When the fire broke out two women were giving birth. The babies are alive. God, people get killed here, they die here, they disappear, things go up in flames here, and out of the flames, new lives are born.

From *Zlata's Diary* by Z. Filipović

PACE AND DESCRIPTION

- In a small group, pick out key words that describe the horror of the war in Zlata's diary. How does she emphasise her feelings? Discuss her use of punctuation.
- Zlata often uses short sentences. What is the effect of this, and what does it show about how Zlata is feeling?

Dear Diary

- Page 6 of your diary could be an entry about something which you particularly remember or feel strongly about:
  'The events of today really changed things...'
  'On the news today I heard...'
  'I vividly remember when...'

CATHERINE'S DIARY

Sometimes, diaries deal with really uncomfortable, intimate, personal feelings.

Catherine Dunbar suffered from anorexia nervosa from the age of 15 until she died, aged 22. She left behind a collection of diaries and letters which her mother, Maureen, wanted other people to read.

7 July 1981

Mood: Mixed. High/Low
Weight: 30.2
Breakfast: $1^1/_2$ Kit-Kats, tea.
Lunch: $1^1/_2$ Kit-Kats, tea, soda water, 3 cinnamon.
Supper: 1 sausage roll, 1 pasty, potatoes, cheese dish, tea.
Binge: Supper incorporated, 2 boiled eggs, bread, Dutch crisp bakes, moussaka, cereal, 2nd moussaka, potatoes, Dutch crisp bakes, bread, sweets.
Laxatives: 110 approx.
Remarks: My binging went on the whole evening and when Mummy and Daddy arrived home I still had not finished. I don't feel that I managed to get it all up. Hence, what will my weight do tomorrow?

23 July 1981

Mood: Fair.
Weight: 31.4
Breakfast: 1Kit-Kat, tea.
Lunch: 2 cinnamon, 2 cheese, Kit-Kat, Fresca, tea.
Supper: 3 sausage rolls, cheese dish, Kit-Kat, tea.
Binge: Marmite and mustard on rye bread, French toasts, Frosties.
Laxatives: 115 approx.
Remarks: Daddy was away tonight. I binged, am feeling low but cannot cry to ease it.

Monday, 4 January 1982

I woke up at 6.15 and went through my normal ritual of getting up, having my breakfast and reading the paper. I was really prepared to go into hospital today, I had got everything ready and everyone has been so fantastic in helping me prepare for it. I am so scared tonight because I did not go and have lost my nerve for going in. If only I could have smoked, but I couldn't possibly have given that up as well as my laxatives, Kit-Kats, routine and freedom. Worst of all I know deep down that I will never be able to eat or face gaining weight, but at least had I gone, I would have felt I had given it a try. I can just see how everything is going to go now. Daddy will never smile or do anything to please me. He will pressurise me and I cannot face that. If only he would understand that it really is not my choice that I should die, but that I am trapped. In the forefront of my mind is the fact that I know I can never eat and gain weight. I am just fooling myself.

From *The Diary of Catherine Dunbar*

PRIVATE AND PUBLIC

What did you think about as you read Catherine's diary? What do you think about reading someone else's private diary? There are things that you might write for yourself that you would change if you wrote for others.

- Look at the list of things that you might write about in a diary. Copy the columns marked 'private' and 'public', and make a note explaining the difference between the way in which you would treat each topic.

Topic	**Private**	**Public**
Feelings about self	*Willing to reflect. Imagine how others see me.*	*Treat with caution. Some feelings too private.*
Being a success		
Being a failure		
Embarrassing situations		
Relatives		
Other people		

Dear Diary

- Write your own intimate diary entry. It could be about anything – boyfriends/girlfriends, family situations, best times/worst times, growing up...

  You probably don't like the idea of anybody else reading this page, so write two versions, one for yourself and one that you wouldn't mind somebody else seeing. The first version could be sealed in an envelope and attached to page 7, whilst the second version becomes page 8.

TRAVELLING IN TIME

In 1722, the author Daniel Defoe used the diary style to write an imaginary journal about London at the time of the plague which swept the city half a century earlier, in 1665.

One of the worst days we had in the whole time, as I thought, was in the beginning of September, when, indeed, good people began to think that God was resolved to make a full end of the people in this miserable city. This was at that time when the plague was fully come into the eastern parishes. The parish of Aldgate, if I may give my opinion, buried above a thousand a week for two weeks, though the bills did not say so many; – but it surrounded me at so dismal a rate that there was not a house in twenty uninfected in the Minories, in Houndsditch, and in those parts of Aldgate parish about the Butcher Row and the alleys over against me. I say, in those places death reigned in every corner. Whitechapel parish was in the same condition, and though much less than the parish I lived in, yet buried near 600 a week by the bills, and in my opinion near twice as many. Whole families, and indeed whole streets of families, were swept away together; insomuch that it was frequent for neighbours to call to the bellman to got to such-and-such houses and fetch out the people, for that they were all dead.

A
JOURNAL
OF THE
Plague Year:
BEING
Obſervations or Memorials,
Of the moſt Remarkable
OCCURRENCES,
As well
PUBLICK *as* PRIVATE,
Which happened in
LONDON
During the laſt
GREAT VISITATION
In 1665.

Written by a CITIZEN who continued all the while in *London*. Never made publick before

LONDON:
Printed for *E. Nutt* at the *Royal-Exchange*; *J. Roberts* in *Warwick-Lane*; *A. Dodd* without *Temple-Bar*; and *J. Graves* in St. *James's-ſtreet*. 1722.

Daniel Defoe is not the only diary writer to have imagined that he lived in a different time. Some have looked to the future rather than the past.

Captain's Log, Stardate 45223.4:

The *Enterprise* has received a distress call from a remote scientific station upon the planet Phaedra in the Xerxes system. The message was from Mikal Tillstrom, son of Dr. Adrienne Tillstrom, a xenogeologist of note. The distress call was patchy and disrupted by some electromagnetic phenomenon, which is not surprising, Xerxes is known for its odd electromagnetic fields. Enough of the message came through, however, to establish that some sort of disaster has overtaken Science Station 146, and emergency aid is sought. Then the message was disrupted and ended.

I have ordered the Enterprise on a course and heading that will take us to Xerxes in a day and a half. Rescue operations are being prepared.

I know Dr. Adrienne Tillstrom, though I have not seen her in many years. She is a fine person as well as a brilliant scientist. I only hope that we can save her and her son from whatever catastrophe has occurred.

From *Star Trek* by N. Archer

HELP

When you imagine yourself as a different person or even a different thing, you are 'adopting a persona'. It is like putting on a mask and speaking through it.

ADOPTING A PERSONA

Consider how some diary writers have adopted a persona, and what that persona is:

DAY 19

She left me naked for a moment in the bathroom in the middle of a nappy change this morning, and I thought I'd have another go at this standing-on-my-own-two-feet lark.

It was a long time before I fell, but the inevitable could not be held off for ever. As usual, I wobbled, my legs gave out and without my nappy as a cushion, my backside took the full impact.

And this time it *hurt*. Really hurt. I hadn't quite realized the vulnerability of a nappyless bum.

I let out a huge bellow and She came rushing in to comfort me.

My bottom was still red and smarting at bedtime. I think I may put off further experiments in standing up for a while.

DAY 23

Back to the supermarket. She was wary this time and pushed the trolley right down the middle of the aisles so that I couldn't grab anything. I concentrated on the stuff in the trolley instead. Decided to eat it. Some of the packaging must have been designed by Securicor, but I made inroads.

I ate three buns, a chunk of Edam, a banana, half a packet of spaghetti, a sachet of shampoo, a lump of butter and a box of the cat's Munchies.

When I say 'ate', of course I don't mean ate properly – I just sort of chewed and slobbered over everything until it looked absolutely disgusting. Except the Munchies. I ate them. I don't know if you've tried them. They are delicious.

From *Look Who's Walking* by S. Brett

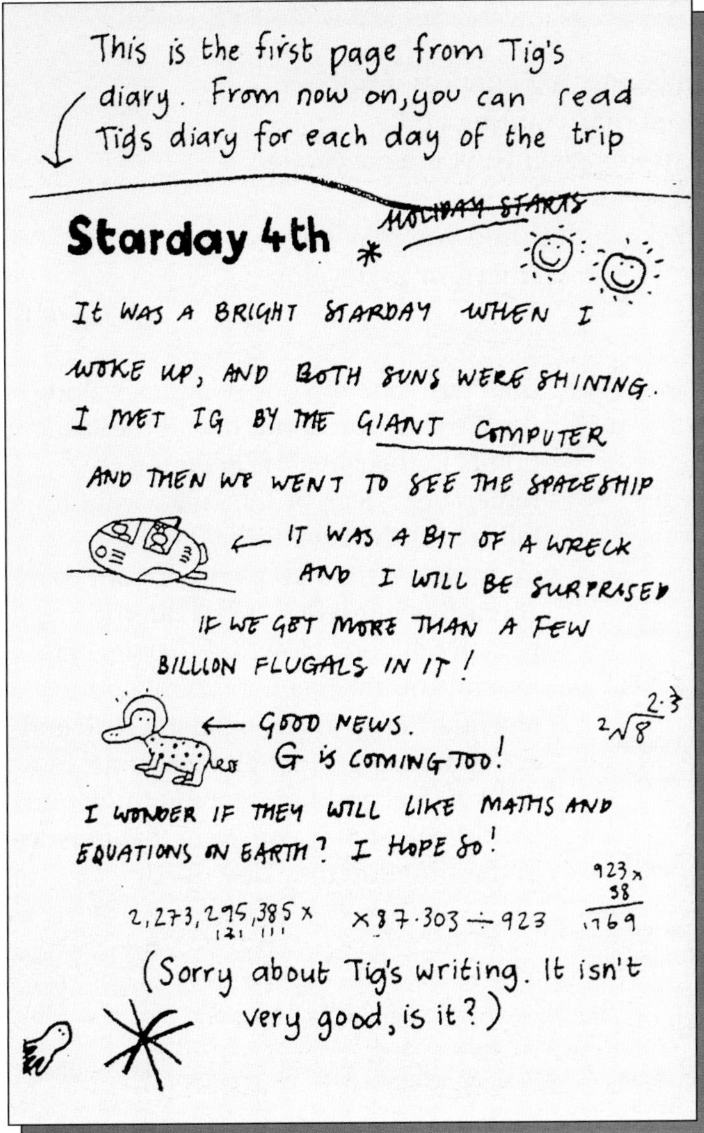

This is the first page from Tig's diary. From now on, you can read Tig's diary for each day of the trip

Starday 4th ~~HOLIDAY STARTS~~

IT WAS A BRIGHT STARDAY WHEN I WOKE UP, AND BOTH SUNS WERE SHINING. I MET IG BY THE GIANT COMPUTER AND THEN WE WENT TO SEE THE SPACESHIP

IT WAS A BIT OF A WRECK AND I WILL BE SURPRISED IF WE GET MORE THAN A FEW BILLION FLUGALS IN IT!

GOOD NEWS. G IS COMING TOO!

I WONDER IF THEY WILL LIKE MATHS AND EQUATIONS ON EARTH? I HOPE SO!

(Sorry about Tig's writing. It isn't very good, is it?)

From *Ig and Tig* by K. Brumpton

A roundish yellow-brown object was shoved under my nose and against my mouth. The saltiness reached my tastebuds and released waters in them. Without further thought, I snapped at the proffered food and crunched it into gooey mash. It was crisp yet oily, full of lovely flavours; it was delicious. I swallowed three in quick succession and shuffled my hindquarters in anticipation of more, my head craning upwards, jaws half open. No more was offered me, and as the figure moved away a funny gurgling noise came from his throat. Disappointed, I studied the ground for any small crumbs that may have escaped my munching teeth. Soon, the floor around me became a very clean area. I gave a little yap at the man above me, demanding his attention. But still he ignored me, and I became a little cross. I pulled at the soft skin that hung over his hard feet (it was a little time before I realised these tall creatures wore other animals' skins and in fact couldn't shed their skin at will).

From *Fluke* by James Herbert

Dear Diary

- Let your imagination run wild! Write a diary entry that is completely different, in which you adopt the persona of somebody or something else in whatever time or place you choose. Do not tell the reader who or what you are, but give plenty of clues so that your identity and world become apparent.

WHAT NEXT?

In this unit, you have read real and imaginary experiences written in diary styles, you have discussed styles of diary writing and brainstormed ideas in your group. Most importantly, you have created your own diary using several different styles and subject areas.

When you have completed all the tasks in this unit, you may have time to do a further project to improve your own diary, or to develop your understanding of the diary form:

- Look back over the diary extracts you have read. Write three or four paragraphs explaining what these extracts have in common and the ways in which they are different.
- Imagine yourself as a young alien making your first visit to Earth. You are part of a fact-finding mission to find out from schools how the Earthlings educate their young. What do you make of the strange lessons, the teachers, the bizarre rituals of assembly, break and PE? Write an alien diary, recording your impressions of Earthling education.
- Collect some recent newspaper reports of an event which interests you. Write two pages of your diary, adopting the persona of someone involved in the event or of the reporter. You could stick photographs from the newspapers into your diary.
- Interview one of your relations, asking them to tell you about one of the turning points in their lives. (They may remember a war, or they may want to talk about their wedding day for example). Write two pages of your diary about this interview. What did the person tell you? How did they feel at the time of the event and how do they feel now? How did the person look and act while they were talking to you? How did you feel and how do you think you would have felt if you were that person in the situation they described?

UNIT SEVEN

Teamwork

In this unit, you will practise speaking and listening in a team where you can work together and support each other. By working in pairs or with different groups you will develop skills as:

SPEAKERS AND LISTENERS

by expressing and negotiating a point of view, and co-operating with others to get things done
by interviewing someone and sharing the information you learn

READERS

by working to strict specifications laid down in each situation
by reading, editing and improving the work of others

WRITERS

by creating a class magazine
by using notes to prompt you in speech and to record the views of others

Are you a confident speaker? Many of us find it difficult to think of the right things to say. It is often easier to speak in a small group than to address a lot of people.

SWEEPING STATEMENTS

A sweeping statement is a generalisation. It claims something as a fact that may not always be true. It is often a sign of prejudice. Here are some sweeping statements.

'The only thing that matters in life is making money.'

'Teachers are out of touch with young people.'

'Young people don't know the meaning of hard work.'

'Computer games numb the brain.'

'Animals make better friends than people.'

- What reactions do you see when people say things like this? The worst thing is to get angry and lose your temper in a slanging match.
- Discuss any experiences you have had of such incidents, and how you have reacted as a participant and as an onlooker.
- What advice would you give to someone about to lose control in this way? In a group, make a list of suggestions, and discuss what you do personally.

Top tips:
Make your points calmly.
Stay polite.

Radio Interview

- In groups of three, think up some sweeping statements of your own, then choose the most interesting one.
- In the following activity, you will prepare a local radio broadcast on that topic and interview the person who made this sweeping statement.
- Decide on the following:
  - Who made the statement? (What type of person? Give her/him a name, age and occupation.)
  - Why and when was the statement made?
  - List all the reasons why the person might hold that view.
  - Think of arguments *against* that view.
- To conduct the radio interview you will need:
  - the interviewer
  - the person holding the point of view
  - the presenter who will operate the tape and introduce the programme.

PRESENTER

- Start the tape.
- Welcome viewers to your programme. (You can give it a name.)
- Introduce yourself and explain the topic of 'Sweeping Statements' and what it means.
- Tell the 'story' behind your sweeping statement.
- Introduce the interview.

INTERVIEWER

- Introduce the guest speaker.
- Ask your guest to explain what led to the sweeping statement.
- Get your guest to explain any views in greater detail, for example by:
  - asking for an example
  - asking them to say more about the last point
  - suggesting how other people might react or reply.
- Challenging their view directly, by saying, for example:
  'Many people would find your views offensive because…'.
  'What might the consequences be if everyone had your view?'
  'But surely…'.
- Give your guest the last word.
- Say thank you and hand over to the presenter who will round up the programme in any way you decide.

PRESENTER

- Thank the interviewer and pretend to move on to the next item.

HELP

Closed questions invite one word answers or a predictable response. E.g. 'Do you really believe that?' begs the answer 'Yes' or 'No'.

Open questions require a longer response. 'Why do you feel so strongly about this subject?' is an open question as the interviewee is expected to explain their views.

Tips for interviewing
- Ask open questions whenever possible.
- Although this will be a prepared interview, try to make it sound 'natural'.
- Listen to each other. Respond to what has been said. Don't simply go on to the next questions, but draw out anything interesting that could be explained further or challenged.

THINK ABOUT IT

Listen to each other's tapes.

- What kind of questions drew out the most interesting answers?
- What makes a good interviewer?
- What makes a good interviewee?

BRACES, FLARES OR DRAINPIPES

Why do we find fashions of the past so funny? One generation thinks that flared trousers and platform heels are great to wear, while another will outrage their parents by piercing belly buttons, tongues and eyebrows.

- Choose an older person you know who will talk to you on this subject. For example, you could talk to a grandparent or a neighbour.
- Make a list of questions which will provide you with information about their lifestyle when they were your age.

1 What was trendy when you were my age?
2 What were you allowed/not allowed to do?
3 Who were your heroes?
4 What did you do after school?
5
6
7
8

Interview this person and take notes.

HELP

- Ask whoever you have chosen to give you some time for an interview. Don't do it when they're busy with something else.
- If you can, tape record the interview, so you can make notes later.
- If you are making notes during the interview, explain that you may need to pause every now and then to note down some information.
- Try to get your interviewee involved in a real conversation. You will find out more this way than asking a long list of unconnected questions. Think of the questions as starters to get them talking.

After the interview

In this activity, you will 'become' the person you interviewed, and a partner will interview you using your own list of questions.

Interviewer

- Explain that you are gathering information to use when you write an article for the local paper about how attitudes and styles have changed between generations.
- Pose each question and use them to draw out your interviewee.
- Then swap roles, and you be the interviewee.

You should, by now, be an expert about the information you gained from your interview. This will help you in the next activity.

You will use the information from your interview to write a newspaper article. It will be about how attitudes and styles have changed between the generation of your interviewee, and your own.

- Try to find some copies of a local paper. Look at the feature articles, rather than the news articles.
- Discuss the language of the headlines. Look also at how interviews are used in direct speech and reported speech.
- Draft your article. It should be between five and eight paragraphs long.

Think about it

Language varies over time and in different situations. Is the language of your interviewee different from your own language? How is the language of the interview different from the language of the news article you have written?

WHAT TO DO ABOUT HENRY

Can you argue a point of view? More importantly, can you compromise in order to settle disputes or make decisions?

This part of the unit deals with a controversial subject – euthanasia – sometimes referred to as 'mercy killing'. It asks you to consider what to do about Henry, a widower of 72 suffering from advanced Alzheimer's disease. It is a difficult matter that concerns many families

ALZHEIMER'S DISEASE

Alzheimer's is a mental disorder that affects part of the brain called the cerebral cortex. Gradually, the sufferer loses their mental abilities. It usually occurs in late middle age or late life. The onset is often gradual and the first manifestation is usually a failing memory. It leaves the sufferer unable to cope with daily life and relationships. The memory can deteriorate so severely that familiar things – places and people – become strange. The personality may change and in time, the person loses control of physical functions. Relatives can obtain help and advice from the Alzheimer's Disease Society, Gordon House, 10 Greencoat Place, London SW1P 1PH; tel: 0207 306 0606.

In a group of 3 to 5, choose to be one of the following:

Mandy – You are Mandy, Henry's youngest daughter and unmarried. You work part-time in a local chemist and have knowledge about and access to pain-killing drugs to allow Henry a simple and painless end. You argue that the doctor should be persuaded to allow Henry to die with dignity.

David – You are David, Henry's only son. You always thought you were his favourite and were very close to him. He always said to you, before he got ill, that should he ever reach this kind of state, he would not want to live. You are very torn between your love for Henry and fulfilling his wishes.

Susan – You are Susan, the oldest of Henry's children. You work for a marketing company in the U.S. and haven't seen the family in five years. You've been called over due to the seriousness of the situation. You are strongly opposed to euthanasia.

Plus any other members of the family who are either for or against euthanasia.

You are all gathered at Mandy's house for a family conference to decide 'What to do about Henry'.

Points to consider:

- Private nursing is very expensive; the family would have to pay for it.
- Euthanasia is illegal.
- Although it is against the law, some people see it as humane – a doctor was recently cleared of murder in a case of euthanasia.
- Nursing Henry at home (bringing in a visiting nurse) would be cheaper, but where would Henry live?
- Henry was in favour of euthanasia.

Role play the discussion they have about what to about Henry. You must decide at the end what the next step should be.

David – you start by explaining how things are with Henry and what a difficult situation you are all in.

Mandy – You continue by saying 'You know, I think we should speak to the doctor about helping Henry to die with dignity…'.

HELP

How to role play an argument

- Forget your own point of view.
- Try to understand how each member of the family might feel about Henry. List the views that the character you have chosen might have. Keep them as 'prompts'.
- Try to persuade the others to your character's point of view.
- Listen to what everyone is saying.
- Don't get cross.
- Look for a consensus (general agreement).
- Look for room for compromise.
- If not, look for a majority (you may not be in it!)

Think about it:

- If opinion is divided – on this or any matter – what can you do? Make a list of possible 'next steps' e.g. ask for someone else's opinion.
- What helps to achieve a consensus in discussion?
- What helps to find a compromise in discussion?
- When are consensus and compromise hard to achieve?
- Discuss your personal views about euthanasia.

Whatever decision you come to, each of you, in role, has to explain your decision to a group of people. They will ask questions so that you have to explain why you came to this decision and what your feelings are about it:

- Mandy to her boss and work colleagues
- David to his wife and children
- Susan to a group of friends.

Take turns to be in role and play the parts of the group.

The Experts

This role play asks you to become 'experts' who have a particular job to do and who won't have the emotional feelings that the family have when considering what to do about Henry.

Doctor – You are the family doctor and very sympathetic towards Henry's wishes to 'die with dignity' but you are constrained by the law.

Representative from the Nursing Home – You feel Henry is not suitable for your nursing home as he will need constant supervision and none of the other residents has Alzheimer's Disease. Your staff is already overstretched.

The Family Lawyer – Henry has made it clear in his will that he does not want to end his days in a nursing home. However, the law is clear about euthanasia.

- One member of Henry's family is represented at a conference of experts, which will be chaired by the family lawyer. If you are playing the family lawyer, start by introducing everybody and explain why this conference is being held. Ask people to speak in turn and then allow the discussion to be more open. Remember to reach a consensus.
- Bearing in mind the family's joint decision, come to a medical consensus about what to do about Henry.
- The roles should now be changed around so that a different member of the family is at the conference and different people take on the roles of the 'experts'.

Now write a written report. Make your recommendations. Explain the decision you have reached.

THE RIGHT TO DIE

Read the following extract from the play *Whose Life is it Anyway?* by Brian Clark. The main character, Ken Harrison, has had a near-fatal accident. It has left him permanently disabled, bed-ridden and unable to do anything for himself, while his brain remains lively and intact. Do you agree with his reasons for wanting to die?

Ken I don't wish to die.

Judge Then what is this case all about?

Ken Nor do I wish to live at any price. Of course I want to live but as far as I am concerned, I'm dead already. I merely require the doctors to recognise the fact. I cannot accept this decision constitutes life in any real sense at all.

Judge Certainly, you're alive legally.

Ken I think I could challenge even that.

Judge How?

Ken Any reasonable definition of life must include the idea of its being self-supporting. I seem to remember something in the papers – when all the heart transplant controversy was on – about it being alright to take someone's heart if they require constant attention from respirators and so on to keep them alive.

Judge There also has to be absolutely no brain activity at all. Yours is certainly working.

Ken It is and sanely.

Judge That is the question to be decided.

Ken My Lord, I am not asking anyone to kill me. I am only asking to be discharged from this hospital.

Judge It comes to the same thing.

Ken Then that proves my point; not just the fact that I will spend the rest of my life in hospital, but that whilst I am here, everything is geared just to keeping my brain active, with no real possibility of it ever being able to direct anything. As far as I can see, that is an act of deliberate cruelty.

THINK ABOUT IT

- In what ways are Ken and Henry's situations similar or different?
- Is there a principle at stake? What is it in each case?
- Why is it important to understand other people's principles?

CREATING A CLASS MAGAZINE

The purpose of this activity is to create a class magazine to appeal to others in your year. Work as a group of 5 or 6 people, operating as a team. You must all agree about the key decisions. This will give you experience of making compromises and achieving consensus.

Agree on the following points:

1 A suitable name for the magazine.

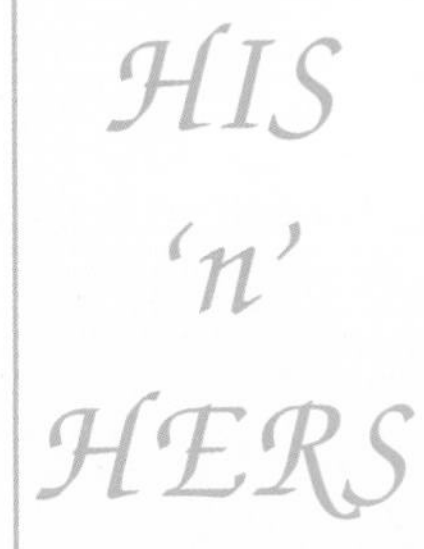

ThE BiZZ

MASSIVE!

2 Choose an image for the front cover. Look at the titles of the magazines on the next page. Can you tell from the front pages who the target audience might be? How do you know?

3 List the items you will have in the magazine. It is worth looking at several different magazines to see what they contain.

4 How you will address your audience. Imagine you are speaking directly to your readers. What impression do you want to give? Do you want to appear cool and trendy? Sensible and mature? Knowledgeable and intelligent?

5 What the feature articles will be about.

6 How long it will be and how many pages will be given to each item.

HELP

FEATURES

Features are articles chosen with the target audience in mind. If you are writing a class magazine for people of your own age group then you will probably want to include articles on Sport, Pop Music, TV and Film, Videos, Fashion, Teenage Concerns (such as Smoking, Drugs, School Uniform, Animal Rights) – anything that you think might interest your readers. Surveys are popular. For example, you could find out how many people smoke or have tried smoking or whether any of your class would vote to get rid of the royal family!

FOR LADS WHO LIVE FOOTBALL
GOAL!
Total Premiership coverage
First for football news
TOTAL FOOTBALL COVERAGE
Every big game sussed and rated p14
RESULTS 'N' REPORTS
Latest Prem matches reviewed
EXCLUSIVE!
Rio
talks England and the Premiership
WIN!
Michael Owen's signed England shirt p98
8 COOL
PLAY BETTER FOOTY
ONLY £1.50
computer act!ve
12 - 25 AUGUST 1999
EVERY FORTNIGHT
Mrs Active
Mr Active
Miss Active
Master Active
Happy family PCs
Buy yourself a PC that suits all the family p38
Exclusive!
Packard Bell Pulsar 900
Best value PC on the high street?
Logitech
WIN!
Internet
free cinema tickets for mizz readers
Life, lads and laughs!
No.375 August 11 - 24 1999 Every fortnight
mizz
£1.30
6 page sleepover pull-out
The juice on Jack
Real life
'Trapped in my burning bedroom'
'No-one believed I was ill'
Win!
VIP tickets to see 911
S Club 7 talk girl
How to look cool in white
SMASH HITS
NON-STOP POP!
WILL SMITH
WESTLIFE
S CLUB 7
FIVE
BSB
TLC
£1.25
AUG 11, 1999
"GUESS WHO WE FANCY!"
Over 50 pop stars confess their crushes!
WHO FANCIES WHO? SPECIAL!
ADAM RICKITT ANSWERS YOUR QUESTIONS!

Roles in the team

Now decide on roles. You can have more than one or work in pairs. At the beginning, everyone will need to join in in the writing. You will need:

An Editor – Your job will be to write the editorial and to see that everyone meets the deadlines that you jointly set as a group. You are like the chairperson and make the final decision on what the magazine will look like. You also spot the jobs that no-one else is doing and make sure they get done. Although this has to be agreed by everyone, you are the boss! You should also write articles for the magazine. You will have to proofread the magazines and make sure there are no errors!

A features editor – Your job is to see that everyone in your group contributes an interesting article for the magazine. You should ensure that the range of articles is varied (not all about football or all about fashion) and will appeal to both boys and girls.

The 'Fun Pages' editor – You are responsible for selecting and writing the quizzes, jokes, competitions and puzzles for your group.

A Layout and Design person – Your job is to see that the articles are hand-written or word processed in an agreed style. You should not have any 'white' space. You need to arrange pictures, advertisements or photographs in an attractive way and ensure that your magazine looks interesting and easy to read. You are also responsible for the magazine's front page.

Extra people in the group can be absorbed as writers and will participate in the general group discussions and decision making.

When you have finished a first draft, get comments, criticism and a check over by at least two other people before you do it in neat.

Your teacher will help you to display or copy your magazine.

WHAT NEXT?

- Research a topic you feel strongly about. With a partner or a group of friends, prepare a presentation in which you express your views on this topic. You could role play some aspects of it, as in 'What to do about Henry'.
- Consider other areas of your school work where you are expected to collaborate, and review the difficulties and the things that help in making it work.
- Discuss how satisfied you are with the final product. What things went well, and what went wrong, in working as a team? What are the qualities which make a successful team? What are the things that get in the way of working co-operatively with others?